Mending and Washing Your Nets

Fishing Lessons from the Disciples

George DeTellis Jr.
with
David Wimbish

P.O. Box 2727
Orlando, FL 32802

MENDING AND WASHING YOUR NETS

Published by NEW Missions
P.O. Box 2727
Orlando, Florida 32802

*This book is dedicated to
the Haitian fisherman who made
the fifth chapter of Luke come alive
and whose perseverance and hope
have given me inspiration.*

Contents

God is Calling You

On January 6, 1983, my family left our home for Haiti with what we could carry on the airplane. (In March of 1982, we had purchased five ocean front acres there for $7,500. The property was located 25 miles southwest of the capital city of Port au Prince, and three miles off the main highway, down a dirt road leading through fields of sugar cane.) We arrived in Haiti with five tents, a small camping stove, a guitar, and as much food, medicine and supplies as we could carry. We purchased some Haitian mattresses on the side of the road on the way to our property.

When we arrived, about two hundred curious villagers came running out to see us. *"Blanc! Blanc!"* they shouted. "The Americans have come! The Americans have come!" We were surrounded by hundreds of children and adults, who began to poke through our belongings, laughing and giggling as we tried to erect our tents. Many of them had never seen a white person before. They had never seen a house made out of fabric. Why were these foreigners here? Did they come to live in our village? Some of them seemed to be afraid of us, and we were afraid of them, too!

We had been told there was more voodoo in Haiti than any other place in the world, and that there was more voodoo on the Leogane Plain than any other place in Haiti.

In the village of Neply, just a short walk away, all the huts looked alike. They were made of mud and grass, and some were painted white. But there was one exception—the house that belonged to the voodoo priest. That house was bright red. Inside, painted on the walls, were pictures of the Loa spirit gods. The voodoo priest had three wives and twenty-one children. In front of his house was a wooden cross, cemented into a concrete base. There, we could see the bloodstains left behind when he had sacrificed a chicken or a goat. Tied to the cross were red and blue strings, and hair from a horse's tail.

It was all very strange, and we were afraid. We were starting to learn the Haitian language, and the government at that time was a cruel military dictatorship headed by the Duvalier family.

We were Christians who had come to Haiti to preach the Gospel of Jesus Christ. We were going to tell the villagers that they needed to repent and give their lives to Jesus. What would the voodoo priest do if members of his village started to become Christians? Perhaps voodoo priests from several villages would come together and attack the mission at night with machetes and try to kill us. Maybe they would try to burn the mission down. Or perhaps they would go to the government and tell them we were political operatives spreading propaganda against the Duvalier family.

As the darkness closed in, we felt restless—then afraid. Each face had become somber. We were alone here, in such strange circumstances. There was no drinking water, no toilet, no telephone, and no electricity. And worst of all, no one to call for help if something terrible happened.

Did God *really* have a purpose in calling us here? Would all our sacrifices and preparations amount to anything? Many voices seemed to whisper in our hearts... *What are you doing? Why have you come here? Why don't you pack up and go home?*

Unless we made a stand for God—not only in terms of territory, but in the ground of our hearts—we knew we might as well turn back.

That night, with our five tents circled around like covered wagons, we lit a campfire. And we made a big choice. Like gold miners, we were going to drive a stake in the land. We wanted to dedicate this land to Jesus in a sincere way. Gathered around our campfire, we took turns with a heavy hammer, pounding a stake into the ground. Together, we shouted out, "In the name of Jesus, we claim this land for the Kingdom of God!" "In the name of Jesus we cast out every evil thing!" "In the name of Jesus we claim the village of Neply for the Gospel." "In the name of Jesus we claim the nation of Haiti for the Gospel." "In the name of Jesus! In the name of Jesus!" And we drove that stake into the ground until it was buried and could no longer be seen.

On that day, January 6, 1983, a mission was started in Haiti. Like Marines, we had taken the beach, and established a beachhead. From there, we would move inland, hut by hut, village by village, town by town, bringing the Gospel of Jesus to the country of Haiti...

Much time has passed since that unsettled night...the night we claimed the ground of our hearts for God. The night we made a significant and bold step, one of many, that has allowed God's vision and purpose to be fulfilled through our lives.

In the intervening years, much has happened. Some of our fears were realized: the hardships of life in Haiti, in primitive conditions, have challenged us in every way. And yet, God's work here has grown stronger every year. Today:

- We are working with 5,000 students in 19 elementary schools.
- We have a high school attended by more than 500 students.
- More than a 100 students attend our Bible and Business College.
- We employ 210 Haitian Christians on our staff.
- We have erected 43 buildings, including a clinic which provides healthcare to people from 57 surrounding villages.
- We've established 10 churches where Haitian pastors are preaching the Gospel.
- All of this has happened despite the fact that between February 1986 and February 1996 there have been nine different governments in Haiti, plus an international embargo of the island, and a U.N. military intervention led by the United States!

Today we generate our own electricity and get fresh, clean water from our own artesian well. Every simple blessing, in the chaos of Haiti, seems like a miracle to us.

This book is written for men and women who are wondering what God's purpose and vision is for their lives. It's written to those who are excitedly seeking, and eager to prepare themselves for a life of faith and adventure—and it's written to those who secretly wonder if they missed God's plan somewhere along the way...those who wonder if they can ever find some higher purpose for being on this planet, when they feel stuck in a deeply-entrenched routine.

Have you ever wondered:

What does my life count for? What's my purpose for living?

How do I break out of the dull routine I find myself in, and experience God's plan and mission for my life?

What about all these common, everyday things I'm doing—at home, at work, at school, in my local church? Are they meaningless, thankless activities? Or could they amount to something in God's great scheme of things?

How do I get out of the "minor leagues" and move into a place where God can *really* use me to further His kingdom?

How do I catch God's vision—and prepare myself, so I can find the deep fulfillment in life that I crave?

If you have asked these questions in your heart, then you have opened the right book! You may be feeling excited and ready to go, or frustrated and passed-by. But whatever your circumstances are right now, I want you to know:

If you make yourself ready for it—and if you take some simple steps—the pathway to a life of godly vision and purpose will open before you.

You see, I know that God has a calling and purpose for every one of us. Our part is to be faithful…to do the simple things, even though they may seem small in our eyes. God's part is to open the way, and do the supernatural, using our simple acts of devotion and obedience to accomplish things that are great in His eyes.

You may not be destined for a far-flung mission field. God's purpose for you may unfold right in your neighborhood, workplace, or even in your own home. But there is nothing greater than knowing and following the path and plan God has for you. *I promise!*

Nearly 2000 years ago, Jesus met some men who were rowing their fishing boat to shore after laboring all night and catching nothing. In many ways, the story of that dramatic encounter shows us how God prepares each one of us, gifts us with skills (that may even seem insignificant in our eyes), and sometimes lets us experience frustration as He prepares to call us out of the ordinary and into the extraordinary. We are going to look at the New Testament story in Luke 5, known as "the miracle catch of fish," in careful detail. God is still in the business of calling everyday people, with the most common of skills. He gives them new hearts full of vision and joy, by calling them to work alongside Him as He brings His mission to pass through their surrendered lives.

Isn't that what you want—to know God better? To hear Him more clearly? To walk closely with Him, fulfilling His best and highest purpose for your life?

A life of vision and purpose is just beginning, and the higher pathway of God's plan is actually unfolding right now in your life and heart.

Let's walk the steps together, and make sure you are ready to follow Him to the greatest life you can know!

One

A Date with Destiny

One day as Jesus was standing by the lake of Gennesaret, with the people crowding around him and listening to the word of God, he saw at the water's edge two boats, left there by the fishermen, who were washing their nets. He got into one of the boats, the one belonging to Simon, and asked him to put out a little from shore. Then he sat down and taught the people from the boat.

—Luke 5:1-3

Early morning is the very best time of day in Haiti, before the sun has risen too high in the sky, and while the ocean breezes are still cool and refreshing. Later on in the afternoon, it's a pressure cooker of heat and humidity. But just after dawn can be delightful—perfect for walking along the beach, collecting your thoughts and getting ready for what the day may bring.

You never know, do you?

That's what I was doing one morning, shortly after I had come to Haiti as a short-term missionary. As I walked along the black sandy beaches created by ancient volcanoes, lost in my thoughts, my attention was suddenly drawn to a commotion a few hundred yards down the beach. There must have been at least 100 people gathered at the water's edge—men, women and children—all excited about something, and all working together on something I could not see.

I walked faster, curious to find out what had brought all of these people out early in the morning. When I got to where I could see clearly what was going on, I saw that two little wooden rowboats were out in the water, about seventy yards from shore. Some fishermen had rowed out, let out a huge dragnet, and were now wading back toward the shore, bringing the net with them as they came.

Many from the village were helping, grabbing the ropes that were connected to the net and pulling it up onto dry land, hoping to bring a large school of fish with it. If there were fish, people in the village would eat well today. If there was only a small catch—or none—some of them wouldn't eat at all.

No wonder they were involved. It really mattered what happened out in those two rowboats.

My anticipation grew as I watched the people laboring together. Over here, a small boy of perhaps seven or eight was tugging and pulling as hard as his tiny body would allow. Over there, a woman who was late in life gripped the rope with knotted fingers, huffing and puffing as she did her part.

My first inclination was to grab the net and work with them. But they didn't really need my help, and I wasn't sure they would welcome it. I continued to watch and began to pray silently: "Lord, these poor Haitian villagers are hungry and needy. Fill their nets, Lord, as you filled the nets of the apostles 2,000 years ago. Give them the fish they need to feed their children."

I watched expectantly as the nets came nearer and nearer to the shore. Finally, the fishermen and the villagers gave one mighty pull, and the huge net came skidding up onto the wet sand.

Empty.

Well, not quite empty. But almost.

All they had caught was a little basket full of minnows, and one tiny shrimp. They politely offered me the lone shrimp, and then divided up the minnows among the women. These would be fried for lunch.

All of that work…for a handful of food. It didn't seem fair. What's more, the fishermen's job was far from over. Their nets still lay upon the beach, and, as each successive wave crashed upon them, they twisted further into the sand. I'd seen the process before. First, they would straighten out each net. Then they'd wash the seaweed, jellyfish and other "gunk" out of it. Laboring in the hot, salty air, they'd use large crochet needles to mend the snags and tears where the net had caught on rocks, seashells, or other objects on the ocean floor. And, finally, they would fold it carefully and pack it away for the next day's fishing.

I walked on down the beach as the fishermen went on working quickly and with great skill. I found myself reflecting on the picture I'd just seen—excitement, focused energy, simple know-how. I thought about how much daily preparation their fishing efforts really took. Fishing isn't a hobby to these people, it's the food in their children's hungry stomachs. I could imagine them washing their nets later in the day, and spreading them to dry in the sun and salt air. I envisioned them searching for small tears, where a net may have snagged on a coral reef, and repairing the damage. I thought: *Such simple skills, such patience and diligence—all focused on one important purpose. Survival.*

And what incredible happiness, what a rush of fulfillment these people must feel on the days when those nets come up full!

Much later, the scene at the beach caused me to think about men and women I know who are aching to find that kind of intensity, happiness and fulfillment, longing to find their purpose in life. We all long to find our reason for being here, because we were made by God to hunger for a higher purpose that gives our lives richness and meaning. Without this deep sense that we are living out the purpose for our existence, something in us turns gray and empty.

Even good Christians, who know they are "called" by God to some higher purpose in life, can feel a bit lost. They can feel eager, but unsure. Or they can feel unprepared to do what they know God wants them to do, and they hesitate. In any case, the sense that they are missing a deep *satisfaction in purpose* leaves them feeling unfulfilled. But it does not need to stay that way.

Before we go further, do you recognize yourself in one of the following "snapshots"?

Looking for a Destiny

Sally is almost 30, a homemaker. Her loving husband, Tom, has a fairly good job, and she's happy that she doesn't have to work because she enjoys staying home with their two kids. She has things pretty good. But then, why does she feel so frustrated? The thought of spending the rest of her life this way is, frankly, frightening. She works hard every day, with laundry, cooking, shopping, housecleaning and doing what she can to meet the needs of her husband and their children. But she wonders sometimes if all of this will really ever count for anything.

Friends tell her that the greatest thing she could possibly do with her life is to raise her children in a godly home. And even though she knows what they mean, she aches sometimes because she wants to do more with her life—to find her own identity. She loves her kids, and she loves her husband, but she wants to be more than a mom and a wife. She knows she has a lot to give, but where should she give it? She's even talked to her husband about the two of them doing something "radical" for the Lord, before it's too late.

You've heard about women whose "biological clocks" are ticking? Well, Sally's "spiritual-clock" is ticking, and she wants to find a way to make a larger contribution to the world. She has spunk, drive, ability and dreams. How does she get on with making those dreams come true?

—⁓—   —⁓—   —⁓—

Ben is 43 and a repairman, with a wife, Shirley, and three kids. They live in a three-bedroom house in a cookie-cutter subdivision. Because the kids are getting older, the house is a little cramped these days, but it will have to do. He can barely afford the mortgage payments as it is. Ben is doing okay in life. He's got a little bit of money stashed away for retirement, plays on the same city league softball team every year, and has attended the same church for the past ten years, where he's an usher every Sunday.

Yeah…things are fine for Ben.

But sometimes he looks in the mirror and wonders how he got to be 43 so quickly. Wasn't it just yesterday that he was playing high school football? Sometimes at night, he'll lie awake in bed, staring at the ceiling, trying to fight the feeling that life is passing him by, and that he's never really done anything of significance. He's worked hard all of his life, and what does he have to show for it?

Ben hasn't talked to Shirley about his feelings because he's afraid that she might laugh at him, pat him on the head and tell him that it's "normal" for a man his age to feel that way. But what Ben really wants is to get rid of this conflict in his head once and for all. Lately, he's been thinking more and more about quitting his job, moving the entire family to the Bahamas and becoming the captain of his own charter boat. Or maybe he'll go back to seminary, get that degree in theology, and start doing something for the Lord that *really matters.*

—ᴡᴡ—   —ᴡᴡ—   —ᴡᴡ—

Joey is 23 years old, a recent college graduate with a degree in business who has been a Christian for about as long as he can remember. He's been going to school for seventeen years and he wants out of this routine. It's time for him to make his mark in the world. But even after seventeen years of school and a college degree, he's still not sure what he wants to do with his life. He feels frustrated, because he knows this isn't how things ought to be. He feels that he should have clear-cut direction for his life, a passion about something. But he doesn't.

Maybe he'll use his degree to land a job with a Fortune 500 company. On the other hand, he's always been pretty good on the guitar, and he knows that you can make more money as a rock star than you can in the business world. Besides, if he could get a good Christian band together, he could do a lot more for Christ than he could ever hope to accomplish as a nameless cog in some corporate wheel. One thing he does know is that he doesn't want to spend his life like his father, who has spent nearly thirty years with the same company, and has very little to show for it.

What Joey really wants is to be respected, to experience the flushes of power and excitement that come when people admire and defer to him. And he'd like to begin right now, thank you!

What is Joey going to do? Will he be like his father? Will he work hard all of his life and get nowhere? That is what is going to happen if he makes the mistake of thinking he knows how to choose the best path for himself. He is at the edge of finding his path to destiny, but he can't do it on his own, with his limited perspective. He needs spiritual eyes and ears, or else he may find himself living a "successful life" of emptiness.

—ᴡᴡ—   —ᴡᴡ—   —ᴡᴡ—

And then there's Ann. She's 57 and has a husband, Herb, who's retired and likes to spend time in his garden. Their kids are all grown up and gone, with children of their own. It makes Ann sad to think that she's not really needed all that much any more. The children don't need her, at least not the way they did when they were small. As for Herb, he's a good guy, but she can't remember the last time he sent her flowers or told her he loved her for no reason at all. She sometimes feels that she's treading water, waiting for The Golden Years to kick in. It also makes her sad to think about all of the experiences she's had in life and all of the wisdom she's gained that she ought to be sharing with younger women, but isn't.

Maybe she should try her hand at writing a book or talk to her pastor about starting a class at church. She thinks it would be great to be sort of a "mother to mothers." Or maybe she should try to be more like her friend Joan, who goes to Europe or Hawaii nearly every year and seems to find fulfillment in travel. She doesn't really know what she ought to do. And meanwhile, the days are flying by.

—ᴗᴗ—   —ᴗᴗ—   —ᴗᴗ—

Sally, Ben, Joey and Ann. Four people like you and me. Four people who feel dissatisfied—who are "fishing around," as it were, for the life of meaning and fulfillment God has for them. What are they going to do? How are they going to find the fulfillment and satisfaction in life that seems to elude them? How are they going to find a way to stop spinning their wheels and actually begin moving down the highway toward personal and spiritual fulfillment?

They may not know it, but God's voice is whispering to them right now. He is calling them to new adventures of faith. He is asking, "Are your nets washed and ready? Then come, follow me, because the adventure is about to begin."

Do you hear Him calling you? Are your nets washed and ready? The blessings God wants to give to you, and through you, are out there, like so many fish in the sea, waiting for you to claim them.

Let your mind go back for a moment to those ancient fishermen on Lake Gennesaret. It was an ordinary night for them—a night spent exactly the same way they had spent many other nights—fishing. They didn't know that in the middle of their everyday routine they were about to meet their destiny. They didn't know they *had* a destiny! And they surely didn't know that God had actually been using their routine to get them ready for a wonderful calling—and that their lives were about to take a dramatic turn.

The meeting with Jesus on the shore of Lake Gennesaret was not a chance encounter. The same is true of your own meeting with the risen Christ. There is something He wants to do through you. Are you ready to do it?

In the pages ahead, we will discover how to uncover your destiny, as we discuss:

- How to make simple changes in your life when it seems that you've just been rowing around in circles.
- What to do when your nets are empty.
- How to find renewed strength when you feel exhausted and you haven't caught any fish.
- Some risks you need to take if you want to catch a boat-load of fish.
- The miracle that can be yours when you learn to follow "the nevertheless principle."
- How to find and build the team that can help you "reel in" the big one.

All of this and more are in the pages to come.

Before we take a look at the great lessons we can learn from the Bible's account of "The Miracle Catch of Fish," take a little time to meditate on the first great truth God wants you to know:

—₥— —₥— —₥—

You have a wonderful destiny that God has planned for you and that you alone can fulfill! You are very important to Him—and important in His plan. If you are yielded to Him, He will work great things through you.

Two

Listening to the Master's Voice

When he had finished speaking, he said to Simon, "Put out into the deep water, and let down the nets for a catch."

—Luke 5:4

One Saturday not long after we had first come to Haiti, my mother was at home alone, when there was a frantic calling of "Madame George!" She was greeted by three women from the nearby village of Neply. "Madame George, come quickly!" they said, explaining that a baby boy had been born in the village and that they needed my mother to come cut the umbilical cord.

"I'm sorry," Mom said, explaining that all the nurses had gone into Port au Prince and that she was not qualified to cut the cord.

"We know God is with you," they said. "You can do it."

They were insistent. My mom finally agreed that she would go and see what she could do. She rushed to the clinic, where she grabbed a pair of gloves, a blade, some clips—everything she thought she'd need, and then she followed the women as they hurriedly led her to a small hut in the middle of the village.

Inside, a young mother was lying on a banana-leaf mat. Her newborn son lay beside her on the mud floor, with the cord still attached. Mom swabbed the cord with alcohol, as she had seen our nurses do many times before. Then she fastened one clip about an inch from the infant's navel, and the other a couple of inches further down on the cord. After that, she took her blade and began cutting.

As she remembers it: "Suddenly my face went white. Blood was spurting from the baby's cord in every direction. One of the clips was obviously defective. I was close to panic. I didn't want to lose my composure, but I could feel my heart beating double time. Grabbing my bag, I prayed that I brought another clip with me. Frantically, my eyes searched the bottom. Then I saw it—one plastic clip! Wasting no time, I snatched it up, then removed the defective clip and replaced it with the new one. *Click!* Immediately it snapped into place, stopping the blood flow."

The baby's life had been saved—or had it? The next thing she knew, several neighbor women moved forward and began grabbing the baby's head, attempting to "shape it" into a pretty one. My mother finally got them to stop, but there were other voodoo rituals they wanted to perform.

One of the women filled a tablespoon with oil and spices. Another woman held the baby's head, and forced his mouth open. Instead of giving the baby to the mother, so she could breastfeed him, they were going to perform what is known as *La Lok*— force-feeding cooking oil down the baby's throat to flush out the digestive system.

Mom turned to the mother and, in a voice that was as calm, and yet as firm, as she could make it, said, "You told me that God was with me and that I could cut the baby's cord. But I will not take responsibility for the life of this baby if you let those woman put that oil down his throat. You could kill your baby by doing that."

There was a long pause. Who would the young mother listen to? Would she heed the voice of this stranger, who was a newcomer to her village? Or would she listen to the ancient cultural traditions of her friends and neighbors?

Finally, the young mother spoke firmly to the older women and ordered them to stop. There would be no voodoo rituals associated with the birth of this child. My mother breathed a silent prayer, which she followed with another prayer of blessing and dedication.

Many Voices

That was only one of many instances during our years in Haiti when we have had to ask the Haitian people to disregard the other voices that are trying to get their attention—the voice of the voodoo priest, the voice of village tradition, the voice of superstition, the voice of fear of outsiders—and listen, instead, to us, as we speak as representatives of Jesus Christ.

Sometimes, as in the story I just told, they listen, and we gain the victory. Sometimes, they don't listen, and we lose them to ignorance and superstition.

I believe there are many voices trying to get your attention right now. But if you listen carefully you can hear, above all the other voices, the clear, strong voice of Jesus Christ.And the Father is saying, "This is my Son, whom I love; with Him I am well pleased. Listen to Him!" (Matthew 17:5)

Will you listen to the voice of God as He begins to direct your steps? Even if He tells you to do something unusual…maybe even risky?

Fishing with Jesus Now

When the fishermen set out in the morning from the shores of Galilee, they never knew what kind of day awaited them. Maybe a day of disappointment, of empty nets. Maybe a day of plenty and success.

That's how it was for Peter, James and John, on that miracle morning.They had no idea that the disappointment was about to turn into the greatest joy they'd ever known. No idea that Jesus was going to challenge them—and that the risk they'd take would change their lives forever.

I can picture them getting ready for work, going through the routine they knew so well. Bored? Perhaps. Maybe even wishing from time to time that there was another way to make a living. I can imagine a conversation between Peter and John:

"Boy, Peter, this old routine really gets to me sometimes. Do you ever think about doing something else with your life?"

"Well, sure…I think about it sometimes. But then again, fishing is really all I know."

And they kept at it, day after day after day, like assembly-line workers, carrying their lunchpails to the factory every morning, or office workers spending their mornings in the carpool lane and wishing there was something more to life, above the mundane routines of this present existence.

Can you relate to the way those fishermen must have felt? The men who set out for a night of fishing on the Lake of Gennesaret had their eyes focused on the routine of everyday life.They didn't know it, but in a wonderful, pleasant way, their destiny was imprinted in their flesh and blood already, so close to them they couldn't see it. They were *fishermen,* and were about to become *fishers of men.* But they needed their spiritual eyes and ears opened to be able to see and hear the workings of God in their own lives so they could begin to comprehend the destiny that awaited them.

Is that true for you, too? Do you know that God has worked into you certain ambitions, desires, abilities and skills? As you learn to listen to God's voice, He will lead you along the higher path He has chosen for you, where you can use your skills and desires in the purpose for which they were created.

Consider the four people we mentioned earlier:

Sally is a warm, empathetic, caring person who could be very effective as a counselor or working in some other capacity with teenage girls.

Ben, because of his stability, faithfulness and example as a father has touched far more lives for Christ than he could possibly imagine.

Joey is bright, articulate and musically gifted. As he follows God's guidance for his life, he has the ability to be a powerful leader and an example for Christian youth everywhere.

Ann has the writing and speaking skills which, if properly channeled, would enable her to be a leader of women in her local church, and perhaps even on the national or international level.

Too often, people think that because they don't have wonderful, obvious or flamboyant gifts and skills, they cannot do great things for God. But there were no extraordinary gifts or skills evident in the men Jesus met on that ancient morning. They were ordinary, unremarkable fellows. There was nothing to mark them as special, or to set them apart from anyone else on the lakeshore that day. And then they had an encounter with Jesus, and their hearts were opened to listen and obey when He spoke.

No Catch

In my mind I can see Peter, standing knee-deep in the water. Even though he was a big, strong man, he and his friends must have been exhausted from their long night's work—rowing from place to place, dropping the nets and then hauling them in, soaked, heavy and empty. They tried over and over again. If there were no fish to be found in this part of the lake, perhaps they should try over there. And after a couple of fruitless hours there, they would row to another location and drop their nets into the water again.

All night long Peter and the other disciples worked, without the slightest bit of success. And finally, before dawn, exhausted and discouraged, they rowed back to shore. After taking only a few moments to rest, they spread their nets out on the beach, and began washing and mending them. At that moment in their lives, I'm sure they didn't want to think about fishing. They had had enough of that, thank you.

Isn't that the way our lives often go? We plod along, putting in the hours on the job, longing for that holiday at the beach, or the long weekend where we don't have to think about our normal day-to-day routine. All the disciples wanted was to get their nets taken care of, and then they were going to head into the city. Some of them were going to go home, to spend some time with their families before they went to sleep. Some of them were heading down to their favorite little café for some lunch. Or perhaps they had some shopping to do.

And then they met Jesus. And despite the fact that they were tired, something stirred in their souls as they listened to Him preach. After He had finished preaching, He turned to Peter and said, "I want you to go back out there, put your nets in the water, and catch some fish."

"Are You Sure, Lord?"

Put yourself in Peter's place for a moment. What would you have done? It's easy to say, "Oh, I would have done whatever Jesus told me to do." But remember, Peter and the rest of his co-workers had never even met Jesus before. They hadn't heard anything about Him. They didn't know who He was. As hard as they worked without results, you couldn't really blame Peter if he had said something like this:

"Are you sure? We've been out there all night, without getting so much as a bite…and now you want us to try again? Look at these nets. Do you know how much time it takes us to get them back into shape after we've been out on the lake all night? And now, after we've spent all this time washing and mending them, you want us to put them back in the water. Sorry, friend. No can do."

I wouldn't have blamed Peter at all, if that had been his reaction. But it wasn't. Instead, he said, in essence, "Well, we've been out there working all night. And we haven't caught a thing. Nevertheless, if you say we should start over, that's what we'll do."

It wasn't a small thing for Peter to row back out onto that lake. But at Jesus' word, he and his companions were ready and willing to do it.

And, because they had spent time washing and mending their nets, they were ready to act when the Master gave them His Word. If their nets had not been ready, the moment would have passed, and they would not have received the miracle God had planned for them. They would have missed their moment with destiny.

I believe that every Christian needs to hear, see and know that God is working in his or her life to bring about specific ends…to fulfill a particular destiny. I don't know who you are, what you do for a living, how old you are, or whether you are married or single. I don't know your race, gender or political beliefs. But I do know that if you are a Christian, God wants to speak to your soul about the wonderful things He has in store for you.

Whoever you are, whatever you do…are you listening to the Lord's voice?

Or do you feel confused by other voices that seem to call for your attention and energy?

So Many Voices

Think for a moment about some of the "inner voices" that are speaking to you today. They are the same voices that were fighting for Peter's attention that morning so long ago on the Galilean lake.

They are:

1) The voice of criticism.

To Peter, this voice was probably saying something like, "You know there are plenty of fish in this lake. But you don't know how to find them. What makes you think that you're going to find them now? When it comes to fishing, you'd make a good farmer. Why don't you give it up?"

This is the voice that keeps reminding you of all the mistakes you've made in life. It tells you you're not worthy.

A friend of mine was crippled by his father's constant criticism during his growing-up years. "You'll never amount to anything," he was told again and again. Today, even though he's married, holds down a good job and, to all outward appearances is doing well in life, this man feels like a failure. Frankly, he drives his friends crazy because he's always apologizing and saying he's sorry, and they don't have the slightest idea what he's apologizing for. Long after he moved out of his parents' home, he is still listening to the voice of criticism.

This voice is constantly telling people that they don't have anything to offer: "You can't sing like Amy Grant, you can't preach like Billy Graham and you certainly don't have the creative talent of Frank Peretti. What good are you?" The truth is, so what if you're not Amy Grant, Billy Graham or Frank Peretti? You have your own talents and abilities that are important to God!

If you are listening to the voice of criticism, you are listening to lies that can cripple you, stunt your spiritual growth and keep you from fulfilling God's plan for your life.

What does God say in response to the voice of criticism? He says:

> "I created you in my image." (*see* Genesis 1:26)
> "I love you so much I sent my Son to die on your behalf." (*see* John 3:16)
> "I have a plan for your life." (*see* Jeremiah 29:11)

God knew everything about you before you were born, even your name! If you are a Christian, your failures and mistakes are covered by the blood of Jesus. You are justified before God, which means that it is "just as if" you had never sinned.

2) The voice of doubt.

This is very similar to the voice of criticism, except that it discredits God, instead of self. This voice would have said to Peter, "I know this fellow preached a great sermon, and there's something special about Him…but what makes you think He knows where the fish are?"

To you, it might be saying, "What makes you think God really cares about you? He's got more important things to do. He's not concerned about your life."

But God *is* concerned about you, and there is nothing more important to Him than helping you find your destiny. I can't begin to understand it, but the Bible tells us that God even notices when a sparrow falls to the ground, and that, "you are worth more than many sparrows." (Luke 12:7)

I find that it is relatively easy for people to believe in a sovereign God. They believe He created the universe. They know there is a Being out there who is all-powerful, who is bigger than the rest of us. But they have trouble going beyond that.

The truth is that the Creator of the universe is a benevolent Father who wants only the best for you. *God loves you deeply*. If it requires a leap of faith to believe that, then go ahead and leap. Believe that Romans 8:28 is speaking expressly to you when it says that God is working all things together for your good.

Think for a moment about the most important relationship you have. God loves you more than that. Do you love your children? God loves you more. How about your parents? Again, God's love for you surpasses your love for them.

I believe God loves you so much that the deepest human love is only a pale shadow by comparison. Whoever you are, wherever you are as you're reading this book, God is loving you right now, with an intense, perfect, unfaltering love. Those who don't understand that God loves them in this way wind up trying to control their own lives, which only leads to failure and disappointment. When you begin to understand the love God has for you, you'll be able to trust Him enough to turn control over to Him, and that's when the miracle begins to unfold.

3) *The voice of selfishness.*

This voice was telling Peter that he had worked hard, he was tired, and he had a right to go home and get some rest. It probably spoke with a touch of resentment and sarcasm, as in, "This Jesus has a lot of nerve to tell you to get back out there and do some more fishing. He must not have any idea how hard you've been working."

In our society, it's easy to listen to the voice of selfishness. Television tells us, "Sure, it costs more, but I'm worth it." Popular books tell us to "look out for number one." And Hollywood often tells us that it's important to be rich, beautiful and to enjoy life to the fullest.

It is often true that the more people have, the more they want to hang on to. For the most part, people in Haiti don't have much of anything. And yet many of them are willing to give. They will invite you into their tumble-down grass-and-stick homes to share a meal with them, even though they may not know when they will eat again.

The late Mother Teresa told of the time in India when she brought a small portion of rice to the home of a woman who had no food for herself or her children. The rice was barely enough to provide one decent meal for this family. The woman took a handful of grain from the sack and poured it into her family's food bowl. Then she took another handful and set it aside. Another handful for the family. And a handful set aside. Finally, Mother Teresa's curiosity got the best of her, and she asked the woman what she was doing.

"I am going to give half of the rice to the family next door," the woman replied. "They are starving, too."

She was willing to share the little bit she had, even though she, herself, was in desperate need.

Scripture teaches that in order to get, you must be willing to give. In order to find your life, you must be willing to lose it.

The Bible tells us about a wealthy young man who came to Jesus asking what he needed to do to inherit eternal life. He was a godly man, because the Bible tells us that he had followed all of God's commandments since he was a boy. But Jesus said:

"You still lack one thing. Sell everything you have and give to the poor, and you will have treasure in heaven. Then come, follow me." (Luke 18:22)

The Bible goes on to tell us that when the young man heard the words of Jesus, "he became very sad, because he was a man of great wealth."

At that moment, confronted with the choice that would make an eternal difference in his life, that young man walked away from Jesus, and, apparently, into the arms of the world. He could have become one of the great heroes of the faith. His name would have been as familiar to us as Peter, James or Moses. His story could have inspired millions of people—the young man who sacrificed everything for the love of God.

But he wouldn't do it. And so today we don't even know his name. He will remain forever anonymous, the pathetic symbol of selfishness—a man who gave up the opportunity to walk with and learn from Jesus on a daily basis, because he couldn't bring himself to part with his earthly possessions.

Before leaving the story of the rich, young ruler, there are two points I want to make:

- I believe God wants you to grow and flourish where you are—as the old cliché says, "bloom where you are planted." At the same time, I believe that He wants you to be ready to surrender everything that gets in the way of following His will. Jesus knew that the rich young ruler's wealth was the most important thing in his life, and He asked him to lay it on the altar. Again, God wants us to be willing to give up anything that stands in the way of our obedience to Him. Who knows? He may be calling you to Haiti or some other mission field. But again, the important thing is to be ready and listening so you can obey Him whenever He calls and whatever He asks you to do.

- I also don't believe any of us can ever get to a state where we're completely unselfish. Self-preservation is the primary function of every entity, and every human being is, himself, the center of his universe. Nonetheless, we can grow in self-giving.

I want to make it clear that I'm not advocating the impossible: to be completely unselfish. When I talk about the voice of selfishness, I mean the inner voice that is calling you to increasing self-centeredness, to put your own needs above the needs of anyone else, to see to it that your needs are met no matter what the consequences might be or who gets hurt.

The voice of selfishness says, "You've been teaching this class for a long time, and no one even cares. No one appreciates it. It's time you did something for yourself. Let somebody else do the hard work."

The voice of selfishness says, "Hey, you've been toeing the line here and getting nowhere. Maybe it's time you took a few short-cuts."

It is the call to increasing selfishness, and that is a voice that no Christian can afford to listen to. To grow in Christ is to grow in selflessness.

4) The voice of limitation.

I'm certain this voice was talking to Peter, telling him that he was already doing everything he could possibly do with his life, and that the last thing he needed to do was to get involved with some itinerant preacher. "You've got a good job, you've got a family, you can't do anything more."

When my dad—George, Sr.—first went to Haiti he was serving as the pastor of a growing church in Worcester, Massachusetts. As a pastor and the father of four children, he had his hands full. What's more, he had no intention of leaving the pastorate and moving to a primitive island.

But when he first went there in 1977 and came face to face with the stark spiritual and physical poverty there, he knew God was calling him to do something about it. In response, he started a feeding program. After that, he made several more trips to Haiti as God continued to draw his attention back to the island and the people there who desperately needed to know God's love.

Meanwhile, Dad was continuing to pastor his church, ministering to his flock in Worcester, washing and mending his nets, waiting on God, and seeking to live in obedience to His will. He remembers clearly the day in Haiti, as he was walking along the beach, when God spoke to him about buying land there and beginning a full-time ministry to the Haitian people. That was the day New Missions was born in Haiti.

My father chose to listen to the voice of God over the voice that said to him, "You have your hands full. You're already doing enough for the people of Haiti. Leave it to someone else to take it to the next step." He could have done just that, but then he would have missed out on the wonders God has worked in and through him, and the rest of our family.

Again, I have to add a word of caution. I am *not* saying that you necessarily need to be doing something more than you are already doing. It is just as likely that you are already trying to do too much, and God wants you to cut back on your commitments. He may be calling you to set aside the things that aren't really necessary and concentrate on what's really important. The voice of limitation tells you that you're already doing everything you possibly can, you can't do anymore and you can't change.

It is just as dangerous to listen to the voice that tells you you're not doing nearly enough and you need to do more. Listening to this voice is an especially dangerous temptation for people who are in full-time Christian service. I have seen so many men and women of God who have burned themselves out by trying to take on more than they were capable of handling.

There is great danger in moving to either one of these two extremes:

- Listening to the voice that tells you you're doing too much.
- Listening to the voice that tells you you're not doing enough.

I suggest that you focus on one thing and learn to do it well. It may appear that New Missions is doing a lot of different things, but we seek to remain focused on what God has called us to do.

The important thing is to be listening to God's leading, as He directs you in whatever it is He wants you to do.

I believe it is only when your nets are kept clean and in good repair that you can hear what God is saying to you. There is something very important about having a "clear channel" with God. If your heart is pure, your hands are clean and your house is in order, then the lines of communication will be clear and free from static.

But if your nets are torn and dirty—if every aspect of your life is teetering and tottering, then how can you hear God when He speaks to you, and how can you receive His blessing?

Only if your nets are clean and repaired will you be able to experience the higher purposes to which He is calling you.

Listening to God's Call

Just in case you still think that God can't or won't use you, let me tell you about Jonas, a boy from the village of Neply who was eleven years old when he first came to us.

Jonas was a *restavek*, which means that he was sent by his parents to live with another family as their servant. (In the Creole language, *restavek* means "to stay with." There are an estimated 300,000 such child-servants in Haiti.) In many Third World countries it is a common practice for poor parents to lend their children into servanthood. Usually these children go to live with wealthy families in the city, where they perform menial tasks. In exchange for their hard work, they get a place to stay and food to eat, although it's often true that the food they get is leftovers. Sometimes these children are physically or verbally abused. And yet, often, parents give up their children because they can't afford to care for them. This was the case with Jonas.

Jonas was from the village of Neply, where his mother was still living with his five younger siblings. He was living and working as a servant in Port au Prince, when a friend from Neply saw him and told him about the mission that had come and started a school in his village. He came and asked my father if we would accept him into the school.

We could see right away that he was bright, ambitious and had tremendous potential. We admitted him into our school, where he excelled. When he finished grade school, we sent him on to a private high school, because we had not yet begun to build our own high school. After that, with our help, he went on to a university in Port au Prince. Today, Jonas is an administrator in our Bible and Business College and at our high school.

He is a top employee, and he is helping us educate the young men and women who, I believe, will help to revitalize Haiti and turn it to the Lord. None of this would have happened if Jonas had not been listening to the call God was placing on his life.

I am certain that many great things will be accomplished through the lives he is touching. And yet he was once considered the lowest of the low…a servant boy. No one looking at him would have suspected it, but God had a destiny for that child, as sure as He had a destiny in mind for the fishermen in Galilee. And He has a destiny for you.

———

You can prepare your heart, soul and mind to meet your destiny by opening yourself up to God again, and that means to begin observing the pattern He has worked into you as He prepares and calls you to a higher purpose.

Three

Working Hard— Getting Nowhere

[Jesus said,]… "Let down your nets for a catch."
—Luke 5:4 (NKJV)

"I know the plans that I have for you," declares the Lord… "plans to give you hope and a future."
—Jeremiah 29:11

…a hope and a future!

*I*magine that God is above you, looking down on the time-line of your life. He can see all those moments that lie ahead for you, when you encounter an overwhelming sense of joy. Those moments when you say to yourself, *I found God's true purpose for me. I'm in it. I'm doing it. I've never felt more fulfilled, at peace, and happy in all my life!*

This is the goal—the moment when your life is more completely in-synch with God's purpose for you—that can become your "faith vision" right now! In a sense, your "vision" for the future.

Now I want you to be careful not to cook up some great vision for yourself, and then ask God to bless it the way you've scripted it. That's a mistake. For one thing, there are lots of turns in the path ahead for every one of us. For another thing, I have learned that the path to God's purpose begins with you and me— that is, with the work He needs to do *in* us, so His plan can be worked out *through* us.

35

For that reason, you need to take a careful look at where you stand right now. Not so much your outer circumstances, as the circumstances of "conditions" that exist in your heart. A clear picture of where you stand right now—in your heart—is crucial in preparing to move ahead in God's plan for you.

Giving It All Up for God

Paul Murdock was a doctor, living in the suburbs of Philadelphia with his wife Tammy and their four children. By every American standard, they were doing very well in life. Paul and Tammy and their kids lived in an elegant old colonial farm-house, complete with its own carriage house and plenty of land for the children to play. Paul had a thriving medical practice, Murdock Pediatrics, which was doing so well that he wasn't accepting any new patients.

Paul and Tammy were well-respected in their community and seemed to be living the good life. Who could ask for more? But in the midst of a life that most people would envy, Paul Murdock was dissatisfied and somewhat disillusioned. He knew that what looked to outsiders like the good life wasn't everything it was cracked up to be.

I remember Paul telling me how deep in debt he was. He said that after paying his bills, if he had enough left at the end of the month to buy a cup of coffee, then he knew he'd had a very successful month. You see, Paul had started his practice in the carriage house of his residence. But as his practice grew, he had to hire more doctors and nurses. He began leasing an office building. He borrowed money to make the practice even larger. After a time, he was no longer Dr. Paul Murdock. Rather, he was "Murdock Pediatrics," with a whole bunch of people depending on him.

As Paul tells it, he was using his riding lawnmower to cut the grass in front of his $700,000 house one day when the thought came to him: "Is this it? Am I going to live like this forever, or am I going to do something with my life?"

Paul's dissatisfaction gave him the inner push to do something more.

It all started when Paul and Tammy came to New Missions on a short-term, one-week missions trip, which was their first foray into the developing world. While in Haiti, they got excited about missions, and the next year, decided to come back for another week. And then for ten weeks! Paul eventually became a member of our board of directors. And God kept leading them further.

Today they are medical missionaries in an Islamic country. Paul will tell you that the missionary life has been tough. This is certainly no life of luxury like the one he knew back home in Pennsylvania. He and his family have been through all kinds of hardships. They've been sick with strange tropical diseases. They've had to cope with a primitive lifestyle that many Americans would find appalling. But they couldn't be happier. They are happy because they know they are doing something important with their lives, and because they know they are doing what God wants them to do!

When You Feel Frustrated

I believe the Bible's promise when it says:

> "Delight yourself in the Lord and he will give you the desires of your heart" (Psalm 37:4).

But if that's true, then why do we sometimes feel frustrated and—let's be honest—miserable? One major reason is this: If we do not use the skills and heart-desires God has given us, as He intended for us to use them, we can fall into a routine that becomes spiritually deadening.

Theresa is a gifted administrator, and she has a wonderfully organized home. But she lets the voice of self-doubt keep her from stepping into the work or ministry role she longs to fill with her gift.

Gary has spent his life—and his talents—amassing a great retirement picture, with a large nest egg. He has let the voice of self-centeredness direct all his attention to padding his own life against the impact of the future, rather than letting God make him a vessel, perhaps for others who need his help.

We can all get so wrapped up in trying to make a living, in surviving from day to day that we lose sight of the big picture. We are like those fisherman, out on the lake all night long, working as hard as we can, but stuck in the rut of making a living and never feeling the joy of working toward a greater goal and greater fulfillment.

I agree with what Bruce Larson says in his book, *Faith for the Journey:* "Sometimes I wish that by some miracle each of us would have the interest on $2 million for the rest of our lives. We'd be in the position of never having to make a living again. We could not hide behind the fact that we are trapped in some mean-ingless job. We would be forced to find out what we really want to do with our lives. We would be free to discover from God our true calling."[1]

Larson also gives five excellent guidelines to help people who want to find out what God wants them to do with their lives. They are:

First, listen to God.

This is the obvious one. If you're interested in knowing what God wants you to do with your life, ask Him. And then, listen to what He says. He may speak to you supernaturally. But it's just as likely that He will speak through circumstances, trusted friends, spiritual leaders, or simply through an intense knowledge that "this is what I'm supposed to do with my life."

Second, claim your uniqueness.

Like snowflakes and fingerprints, you are one of a kind. No one else has your experiences. No one else has your exact abili-ties, skills or training. Larson writes: "I know a woman who is writ-ing books right now featuring handicapped children as the heroes and heroines, which is something that as far as I know has not been done as yet. She has a handicapped daughter and is writing out of some of the pain and the hurt and hardship of her own experience." Each of us has had life experiences unlike anyone else's. God gives us unique eyes to see the world around us and the ability to make our own particular contribution.

Third, be open to change.

"That's the way we've always done it." Any pastor can tell you that those are seven very powerful words. They can be like cold water, splashed on a flame of spiritual revival. Some people resist change at every opportunity, because they are afraid of what it might mean. And that is truly tragic, because what it might mean is a renewed relationship with God and a happier, more fulfilled life.

You shouldn't think that you have to change, but neither should you think that you can't change. Some people excuse their mistakes and failures by saying, "This is me. It's the way I've always been." Just because it's the way you've always been doesn't mean it's the way you have to stay.

Fourth, don't limit your possibilities.

Larson writes: "Don't be discouraged by the fact that you are not a professional, that you don't have credentials. All of society seems to be breaking loose in this area. Someone wrote recently: 'Our society is becoming accustomed to the 28-year-old mayor, the 50-year-old retiree, the 45-year-old father of a preschool child and the 70-year-old college student.' We need to stop thinking we're too old or too young or not qualified."

Fifth, simplify your life in order to pursue your vocation.

As I mentioned before, some people are overcommitted, trying to do too much. If this is you, then I suggest you sit down, make a list of your current activities, and ask yourself how many of them are really important to you. How much of what you're doing is propelling you toward the goals you want to accomplish, the things you really want to do? You may be surprised to find that you are involved in a number of activities that could be eliminated from your life without causing you any great harm. As Miller says, "Something may have to go. Make a decision to do those other things less often, that you may do more of the thing God has given you to do."[2]

Discouragement vs. Dissatisfaction

When you have been working hard, but getting nowhere, it's easy to become discouraged.

When that happens, it's easy to give up.

And if you give up, you may miss the miracle that God was about to give you.

Have you ever heard of Elisha Gray?

No? He invented the telephone.

What? You thought Alexander Graham Bell invented the telephone? He did.

Before I get you thoroughly confused, I'd better explain. Gray and Bell were contemporaries, who were working on their inventions at the very same time. But because Gray became discouraged for awhile, setting his work aside because he couldn't seem to get it right, Bell got to the "finish line" first. That's why we have "Bell Telephone" instead of "Gray Telephone," and why almost everyone knows the name of Alexander Graham Bell, whereas very few people have ever heard of Elisha Gray.

Discouragement is a bad thing. It means you are giving up on faith and hope and giving in to the fear that life's obstacles have won. Then you give up, when you ought to keep pushing ahead.

Dissatisfaction, on the other hand, is not necessarily a bad thing. It may be the finger of God, stirring your heart so that you can break free of your routine and accomplish greater things for Him, and thereby find the personal satisfaction you have always wished you could find.

Getting Water from the Rock in Haiti

When discouragement comes to you, whatever its cause, I want you to know that God has the answer for it. And by faith, you can find it.

Discouragement is something we have had to battle many times during our years in Haiti. First of all, it would be an understatement to say that a few people thought we were crazy when we first went there. Some of the land was swampy. There was no electricity. And, most importantly, there was no clean water. The closest clean-water well was seven miles away, and we had to spend hours every week hauling water to drink.

We had begun collecting rainwater from our roofs into a cistern. This was used for washing clothes and cooking, but it was too bitter to drink. For three years, we bathed in the stream that ran alongside our property. We often arose early to bathe before women began washing clothes upstream, which made the water milky from the soap they used.

A well had been attempted the first year New Missions was in existence. Mennonite missionaries had drilled down about 100 feet and hit only mud water. For the next two years, we tried to make do with water pumped in from a nearby stream. We'd filter it and add chlorine, and we'd get it clean enough for bathing, but it still wasn't fit for drinking.

Because our work was growing we were facing ever-greater needs for clean drinking water. We had thousands of children in our school, which meant we needed a lot of water—much more than we could possibly haul back from the nearest fresh-water well. So after years of traveling miles every day for water, we asked the well-drillers to come back and try again. This time we picked a site that was even further from the ocean. Even then, the well-drillers were not optimistic. But because we were persistent, they finally agreed to give it one more shot. My father felt led to a certain spot, so the rig was placed there.

During the time we were drilling this new well, there were 16 missionaries at our compound praying around the clock for success. The drillers themselves also were Christians, so before starting work for the day, they also bowed their heads and asked God to give us a "good well."

All through the day, prayers continued. Some had enough faith to ask God for "a gusher."

We drilled down one hundred feet.

One hundred and fifty. One hundred and sixty.

At one hundred and sixty-five feet, the drill hit bedrock.

There was no water. Not so much as a drop.

That was where the drilling stopped at the end of the day, and you can imagine how discouraged some of us were. We were all trying to hang onto our faith, but some were barely hanging on by their fingernails. After all, we had tried before and failed. What made us think God was going to give the miracle this time? Some people, I'm sure, felt like the Israelites who complained to Moses, "Did you bring us out here to die in the wilderness?"

You know, we could have started a mission school in the capital city of Port au Prince. There, we could have had running water and flush toilets. We could have had electricity to run air conditioning. And if anyone was hungry, we could have driven down the street to Kentucky Fried Chicken. Instead, here we were, miles from nowhere, without so much as clean water to drink. Still, my family knew beyond any doubt that we were exactly where God wanted us to be, doing exactly what He wanted us to be doing, so we knew He would be faithful. Even if the well drillers didn't hit water, we knew that He would supply it in some other way.

We asked the drillers if they would keep going, just a little further, even though it seemed futile. They agreed to give it one more day.

It was very slow going, drilling through that solid rock. Another ten feet, then twenty. Nothing.

And then, at one hundred and eighty-five feet, something wonderful happened! They broke through that rock and into an underground river of fresh, pure water. And suddenly, we received exactly what we had been praying for—a gusher! Water erupted out of that well and begin to flood the entire mission compound.

What had happened? God had given us a miracle. In a place where there was no water, God had suddenly given water in abundance. We had discovered an underground aquifer trapped beneath rock. And it sent up an artesian well of spring water, sweet, cold and delicious.

It wasn't long before people all over Haiti heard about this mighty miracle God had done. Villagers came from all over to see it for themselves. People from development agencies came. People from the Haitian government came. And it turned out that because we had been persistent, we had discovered a clean water source for dozens of villages in our immediate area.

Today at our compound in Haiti, we have a well capped with a four-inch pipe, and when we open it, water sprays out of that thing like a fire hydrant. It's enough to knock you over! We have flush toilets and showers, and a number of spigots where you can get a drink of clean water any time you want. We don't have to have pumps. The water just flows out under its own pressure.

And if you ask the Haitian people where that water comes from, they will tell you that it comes from God—that it was a miracle. And you know what? They are absolutely right.

Only faith led us through discouragement to blessing.

When You Are Struggling

Discouragement occurs when you have been doing the same thing day after day and feel that you're not getting anywhere. When a person is discouraged, he or she feels like giving up and letting someone else do it. Discouragement is one of the most effective weapons in the devil's arsenal. He especially loves to use it against Christians who want to serve in the Kingdom of God to get them to quit before they see the life of purpose and service that God is planning to give them.

Were those fishermen discouraged after fishing all night without catching anything? I'm sure they were. But they listened to Jesus and wouldn't give up. Not only did their circumstances change, their *spirits* changed. Discouragement was washed away and replaced with excitement and joy.

If you feel certain that you *are* doing what God wants you to do, then don't let anything dissuade you from it, even if you've had your "nets" in the water for a long, long time and haven't seen big results. The God we serve is a God of power. In time, you will see Him move, and He will not leave you disappointed!

Dissatisfaction often comes at the point of greatest achievement. It is when things are going well, or when you are on the verge of some great breakthrough, and you suddenly look around and say, "Is this all there is?" Dissatisfaction is what happens to the businessman who finally makes that million-dollar deal and then realizes that it didn't make him happy after all. He looks around and says, "What's wrong with me? I ought to be thrilled, and I feel so bad." That person has been hit with the realization that there is more to life than big deals, corner offices and bonuses. I believe that dissatisfaction is God's way of telling us that we are not necessarily doing with our lives what He has called us to do.

Were those fishermen dissatisfied? The Bible doesn't tell us, but they must have been. It wasn't their destiny to spend their lives trolling that lake, looking for fish. I believe that inside each of them was a feeling that said, "This isn't what I was born to do. I was born for something greater."

And sure enough, they *were* born for something greater.

How about you? Were you born for greater things? Are you doing what God wants you to do? If you aren't, then you may feel dissatisfied, no matter what other successes in life may be yours. And if you do feel dissatisfied, then get ready. It's time for a change!

———⁓— —⁓— —⁓—

> *Say no to discouragement. But pay close attention to your dissatisfaction. It is often the finger of God stirring your soul, getting you ready for the new thing He is about to do in your life.*

Four

When Your Nets Are Empty

Simon answered, "Master, we've worked hard all night and haven't caught anything...."

—Luke 5:5

*H*ow do you suppose the disciples felt after fishing all night long, and coming back to shore with their nets empty?

I'm sure they were disappointed, discouraged and frustrated. It's a difficult thing to work all night long without anything at all to show for it.

But I know something that's even worse: Realizing in your old age that you've spent your whole life chasing after an illusion, and that your nets are empty.

What a tragedy to go through life thinking you are constructing mighty castles that will stand for centuries, only to find, the first time the tide comes in, that they are made out of sand, and are easily washed away.

It is said that a reporter once asked the great playwright George Bernard Shaw this question:

"Mr. Shaw, you have been wined and dined by all of the greats of our generation. They all aspire to your friendship, and you know them well. If you could be reincarnated and come back as some other famous person of our time, who would it be?"

Shaw didn't have to think about it.

"If I could relive my life in the role of any person I desired, I would want to be the man George Bernard Shaw could have been but wasn't."[3]

George Bernard Shaw was a brilliant, creative man who produced many wonderful plays. And yet as he looked back on his life, he saw that his nets were closer to empty than they were to full, because he had not done as much as he could have with the talents God gave him.

What do you see when you look at your life? Are your nets empty? If they are, it is not because you haven't been given the tools you need to fill them. Believe in yourself. Believe in God. Move out in faith, and watch those nets swell with fish! I urge you not to be like George Bernard Shaw, looking back on your life and saying, "I could have...but I didn't."

If you're going through a time when it seems to you that your nets are empty, here are some important things to keep in mind:

- If God is on your side (and He is), then it doesn't matter who is against you!
- You need to be a part of something bigger than yourself.
- Life is full of losses. Making mistakes is part of the learning process.
- You need to know you are important to God.
- You may need to change your vantage point.
- When life gets challenging, you can relax and let God handle it.

Let's take a closer look:

God Is for You:
It Doesn't Matter Who's Against You

One night, not long after we came to Haiti, we went to a small village where we set up some lights and a microphone, and my father began to preach. As always, a crowd quickly gathered to hear him preach in their native language about the love of Christ. I don't remember how many people came forward that night when Dad gave the altar call. I know there were several. But only one of them stands out in my mind. She was a little girl, a child in a ragged hand-me-down dress. She looked like a tiny ebony doll, and she was weeping as she came to the altar, so touched was she, by the thought that the Son of God had given His life for her.

Her name was Vania, and we didn't know at the time that she was the daughter of one of the most powerful men in the village—the voodoo priest. He was very unhappy that his daughter had given her life to Christ, and before Vania even returned home at the end of the service, he confronted her. Pointing his long, crooked finger at her, he told her that if she did not renounce Christ, "You will never get anything from me. The only thing I will ever buy for you is a coffin."

Even in the face of this threat, little Vania would not change her mind. She shook her head shyly, did not show the slightest sign of disrespect, but she would not back down. She would not turn her back on the One who had given His life for her.

To understand what she was giving up, you have to know that the voodoo priest is often the richest, most powerful man in the community. His house is usually one of the best in the village. He has more land. And, because people pay him for his services such as placing curses, removing curses and so forth, he has more chickens, goats or pigs than others in the community. There is prestige associated with being a member of his family. For the sake of Christ, Vania was turning her back on all of that.

Besides, Vania believed that to risk her father's wrath was to risk her life. As far as she knew, he could have sacrificed a few chickens on the altar in front of his house, mumbled a few magical words, and turned her into a cow or a goat to be sold at the local market.

And still, she would not turn her back on Christ.

To the non-Christian, it would appear that Vania was giving up much: the strength and safety of her place in the family; the security of material possessions.

But Vania knows that what she was giving up was nothing at all compared to the riches she received when she became part of God's family. She was exchanging a way of life that was like ragged and empty nets, yielding nothing, for a way of life that was new, strong, a full-catch of blessing.

Shortly after she accepted Christ, Vania enrolled in our school. Over the years, we have had the privilege of seeing her grow up, and her faith has never wavered. She has blossomed into a beautiful young woman who serves the Lord with tremendous joy.

It doesn't matter at all who or what might be aligned against you. It's only Who is on your side that's important!

Be a Part of Something Bigger Than Yourself

I believe that one of the reasons some people are running around with empty nets is that they do not see themselves as part of a larger whole. Instead, their vision is turned inward, focused on themselves. When you turn inward you die.

I have seen a poster that says, "No man has done anything until he has become part of something larger than himself."

I've also seen the truth of that statement demonstrated many times in the lives of those who come to Haiti to work with us there. Haiti is desperately poor. From the air, as you're flying over the island, it looks like a tropical paradise. It is lush and green, with many streams and rivers. Here and there, you'll see a little grove of palm trees with a cluster of little houses nearby. It looks idyllic, the sort of place where Gilligan and the Skipper could happily live out their retirement years. But when you get on the ground and see the poverty of the people who live in those little houses, you discover that life in Haiti is anything but idyllic.

And yet, time and again, I have seen excitement sparkling in the eyes of new arrivals. They are not at all disheartened by the poverty or a first-hand look at the primitive lifestyle that will be theirs while they live on the island. They feel that they are part of a larger movement, a revolution that is going to change the island through the love of Christ. And because they see the potential that exists here, they feel as if their nets are full, rather than empty.

Know That You're Important to God!

If you think God can't use you because you're inadequate in some way, you are in good company! Do you think you're too small, weak or insignificant, or that you're not smart enough or good-looking enough for God to use you? If any of these self-doubts are holding you back, you may need to re-read the life stories of some of the great heroes of the Bible.

What did Moses say when God chose him to lead the children of Israel out of bondage in Egypt? Wasn't it something like this?

"I really think you ought to choose somebody else, Lord. After all, I get tongue-tied, and Pharaoh will never take me seriously."

Moses saw himself as weak and insignificant, but God saw him as a vital part of His plan to release the Israelites from bondage, and to establish them as a mighty nation.

And then there was Gideon, whom God chose to lead a rebellion against the oppressive Midianites. Gideon's reaction was to be even more self-deprecating than Moses. "You can't mean me, Lord! I'm the most insignificant person in the most insignificant family in all of Israel!" But God *did* mean Gideon, and he became a great general who freed Israel from an oppressive occupation.

Even if your nets seem to be empty right now, remember that you are important to God. He wants your nets to be full.

Do You Need to Change Your Vantage Point?

The Orlando area is booming. Big businesses are relocating here on an almost daily basis. The population is soaring. Property values are high. It is America's number one vacation destination.

And yet, I've seen old-timers shake their heads with regret as they recall the days when most of this area was nothing more than cow pasture. If only they had known the value of the land they were sitting on. But they didn't. It took outsiders— Hollywood executives, and businessmen from Canada and England to see the value of this central Florida community.

As far as I'm concerned, I believe that the locals were so close to the palm trees, they couldn't see the coconuts. In other words, they needed to change the way they looked at things.

If your nets seem completely empty right now, perhaps it's because you're not looking at them from the proper perspective, which is from God's perspective.

Remember that things which seem to us to be of little or no value may be of great importance to God. Conversely, things that seem to us to be of great importance may be virtually worthless in His sight. In everything we do, we should ask God to give us His perspective, the eternal perspective, so we are not weighed down or distracted by things that may seem significant today, but which may appear as trivial tomorrow. This should be our constant prayer: "God, help me to see what is really important!"

Perhaps you have heard the poignant story that was often told by Brooks Adams, the son of former Ambassador to Great Britain, Charles Francis Adams. On one occasion when Brooks was a boy, his father decided to take him fishing. Because the ambassador was a very busy man who seldom had time for his son, Brooks saw the fishing trip as a pivotal event in his life. He recorded in his diary that he had "spent the day fishing with my father; it was the most glorious day of my life." As a man, he often referred back to that fishing trip as a life-changing event.

Years later, as Brooks was going through his father's possessions after the man's death, he came across a journal for that same period. When he looked up the entry for the date of that life-changing fishing trip, he was crushed to read, "Spent the day fishing with my son; a wasted day."[4]

What a tragic misperception of the worth of an event. To the son, an inspiring occasion. To the father, a waste. If that father could have seen that fishing trip from God's perspective, he would have known that it was one of the most important days of his entire life. But he couldn't see it that way, and he missed it.

Do you remember how your perceptions changed and shifted when you first came to believe in Christ? All of a sudden, you saw that life had meaning, that it was not a random series of miscellaneous events. You understood for the first time that good eventually will triumph over evil. You also saw that you had hope, not only in this life, but in the life to come. You knew that in spite of your sinful nature, you had been declared "not guilty."

You may be able to think of many other ways your thinking changed when you became a Christian. But sadly, as time passes by, it is easy to gradually slip back into the old way of looking at life. If you feel that's happening to you, ask God to help you get excited all over again about what Jesus has done for you!

As we labor among the extremely poor of Haiti, it is vitally important that we see things from God's point of view, that we not let hope give way to hopelessness. We constantly must ask God to help us see our work through His eyes. We have to see the victories. Only as we look through His eyes can we see that the nets are getting full. All too often, as we look with human eyes, we can only see what remains to be done instead of what has already been accomplished.

In one of his early newsletters from Haiti, my father wrote these words:

> One evening as the sun was setting, I walked to the school and sat outside the *chacoon* (a round type open-porch building), chatting with a few high school students. As we talked, they began expressing their

frustration living in a poor country. "We are suffering. There is nothing we can do. Our life is no better than the animals. Our hope is that this life will pass and we will go to be with Jesus."

For me, these were very hard words. I have always lived in the belief that good things were happening and my outlook for the future has always been bright and positive. But then I have never really been poor.

Believe me, after living with the poorest people in the western hemisphere, I have learned that there is nothing glamorous about being poor. The poor feel trapped. They do not have the choice of food, housing, travel, education or employment. They feel locked in and powerless.

The Gospel has "lift." When people come to personal faith in Jesus, their lives will be changed. God is a God of blessing. Israel was promised full barns and victory over her enemies in return for serving the Lord. We are spiritual Israel....We need to preach and believe that those nations that make the Lord their God will be blessed.

We have the promise of heaven. We also have the promise of our God working in the present, changing, improving and lifting our lives.

We labor in the knowledge that God has sent us and in the belief that His Word can change the world.

Relax and Let God Handle It

Leanne has felt the need to be trained in Bible and counseling because she wants to work in crisis pregnancy intervention. She is finding it a challenge to balance the demands of a home life with three kids and the demands of a two-year college program. Sometimes she lets the stress get to her, until she remembers that prayer and the counsel of her pastor led her on this course. Then she decides all over again to relax and let God help her balance her time as she steps up to God's call on her life.

At 33, Rick quit his job as a newspaper reporter and went to seminary to study for the pastorate. He had been thinking about it for several years, and then when circumstances and the counsel of Christian friends seemed to point him in that direction, he quit his job, packed up his family, and headed back to college.

Now, as he tries to support his wife and child with a part-time job and, at the same time, master courses like Greek and homiletics, he sometimes feels like he's going to explode. Every so often, he has to stop, take a deep breath and remind himself that he knows he's exactly where God wants him to be. Then he can relax and leave everything in the Lord's hands.

What about you? Do you ever feel frustrated, exasperated, in a hurry for something to happen, but it just doesn't? I have some great advice for you which you've probably heard before: "Let go and let God."

I have a confession to make.

Rumor has it that young guys don't really want to get married. Instead, they want to "play the field" as long as they possibly can.

Not me. From the time I was 18 years old, I dreamed of having a wife to love and cherish, to be my life's partner. I had a number of romantic relationships, but for one reason or another, all of them fizzled.

Finally, here I was, 28 years old and still single. I didn't understand that at all, and I prayed about it a lot: "God, where is she? Where's the woman who's going to be my wife…the mother of my children?" It got to the point where I was wrestling with God over this, because, frankly, I'm a normal man and I desperately needed a wife! I didn't want to give in, to settle for anything less than a relationship with the woman I was going to marry, but living a single, celibate life was very difficult for me.

Well, guess when and where I found her?

When? I found her when I wasn't looking for her. Where? In Haiti. Now, as executive director of the U.S. office of New Missions, most of my time is spent running things from our office in Florida. I spend some time in Haiti every year, but not as much as in the United States. Well, I went down to Haiti for Thanksgiving in 1989, and there she was. I wasn't even looking for her, and she practically walked right into me.

Paula was a Mennonite girl from Virginia, a farmer's daughter who had come to Haiti on a one-year mission trip. And she got to me immediately. I was 28. She was only 18. But after a few walks on the beach, and a kiss or two in the soft Caribbean moonlight, I knew beyond any doubt that she was the one.

I made another trip to Haiti in January, and decided to fly Paula and my mother home to Massachusetts over Valentine's

Day. On that romantic day, I asked Paula to marry me, and she accepted. After that, she and I stayed behind while my mom went on back to Haiti. At this point, I thought that since Paula and I were now engaged, it would be a good idea for me to meet her parents.

Paula called them and told them she was in Boston with me, and that we were going to drive down to see them. Of course, they were very surprised that she was back in the United States, and especially in the Boston area. She had never been to Boston before, and neither had they.

For moral support, I called my grandparents and asked if they would drive down to Virginia with us to meet Paula's parents. They said, yes, and we all climbed into their Peugeot and drove several hundred miles to western Virginia, where Paula's parents were dairy farmers.

It was quite a clash of cultures. My grandparents were city-bred Italians in their 70s. Paula's parents were salt-of-the-earth Mennonites living far back in the hills near the West Virginia border.

I wasn't sure how they were going to feel about me. After all, they had sent their daughter off to Haiti to be a missionary, and here she was, coming home to tell them she was engaged to the son of the mission's president, and I was ten years older than she was!

When we arrived, they were very happy to see Paula. But their happiness was overshadowed by their curiosity as to why we had come and what was going on. But I wasn't ready to tell them yet.

It was the next night, as we were sitting up late talking, that I finally told Paula's father that I loved his daughter and wanted to marry her. I didn't really ask for her hand, as much as I simply told him we were going to be married. I noticed immediately that his rocking chair started rocking a lot faster than before. He wasn't happy.

"What's your hurry?" he asked.

I thought I could see suspicion in his eyes.

I explained that we weren't going to be getting married immediately but would wait until September.

I think Paula's mom and dad were both relieved that we weren't really rushing things. Before we left their home, they prayed with us, asking God's blessings upon us as we made our future plans. I realized that I was marrying into a terrific family.

A few days later, Paula had to go back to Haiti without me. I saw her again in March, and then in June. On September 1, 1990 we were married. Now it is almost eight years later, and we have two terrific children. I'm so glad I waited for her!

I believe there's an important lesson to be learned from this: If you've tried and tried and tried and you just can't seem to get it right, it's time to relax, turn it over to God, and let Him do it for you. Whatever it is that you're trying to do, He's better at it than you are anyway!

That doesn't mean you won't make some mistakes along the way. But so what? You can learn something from every failure, if you have the right attitude.

It is said that Thomas Edison tried and failed at least 1,000 times to invent the electric light bulb before he finally got it right. When an acquaintance asked him if all of the failures didn't leave him feeling discouraged, he said, "Not at all. Every time it doesn't work, I've learned one more way not to do it."

What an attitude! No wonder Thomas Edison was such a successful inventor.

As we turn our thoughts back to the ancient fishermen, who had come in with empty nets after a long night of fishing, remember the story doesn't end there. They had failed on their own, but there was Someone else who would enable them to succeed beyond their greatest expectations. All they had to do was listen to His voice, do what He told them to do, and watch those nets swell and fill with fish!

We find our purpose in life only when we get help from beyond ourselves, from a higher perspective, and from the voice of One who speaks from eternity into time.

Five

Ready for the Challenge

*God is not unjust; he will not forget your work and
the love you have shown him as you have helped his
people and continue to help them.*
—Hebrews 6:10

$\mathcal{E}$ight o'clock, Sunday morning in Springfield, Massachusetts, and I'm lost. Also, starting to sweat.

I'm supposed to speak at a church service that starts in half
an hour. I've got the directions, but right about now, they're not
making much sense.

My wife, sitting next to me, gives me an encouraging smile.
She reaches over and pats my hand, letting me know that everything is going to be fine, but I don't think so. Something about
that speeding ticket a few miles back that let me know this isn't
going to be my day.

The kids, in the back seat, are getting cranky because we've
already been in the car for more than hour. I don't blame them.

Have you ever had a day like that? Fifteen minutes after you got
out of bed, you were ready to crawl back in and pull the covers up
over your head. Well, I've had enough of those days to recognize
when one is on its way, and this was shaping up to be a *doozy*.

Wait a minute. I remembered I had the pastor's phone number. I called him on my cellular phone and he said he'd send one

of his deacons out to guide us to the church. As it turned out, we got there just in time for the service.

Seeing the church didn't help to ease my mind. It was an old run-down building smack-dab in the middle of the inner city. Sixteen people had come to hear me speak at the 8 o'clock service—including my family!

If you've done any public speaking, you know how disheartening it can be to get up in front of a large auditorium and see a handful of people sitting there.

Lord, I prayed silently. *I worked so hard on this sermon and there's nobody here to hear it. I'm going to preach my heart out, but I've got to tell you, I'm disappointed.*

My inclination was to suggest that everyone go out, get something for breakfast, and then come back for the 11 o'clock service. But after thinking about it for a minute, I decided that wouldn't be a very nice thing to do, so I cleared my throat and began to preach.

That morning I found out that God doesn't care how big the crowd is. He's not necessarily into numbers. He's into changing lives, touching hearts with His Spirit. And that morning, as I began to preach, the fire of God fell on those few people spread out in that huge auditorium.

People were crying and praising God. They seemed to be hanging on my every word. The entire service was a blessing. When it was over, there was no doubt in my mind that we had all been in the presence of God.

Eleven o'clock service. Same thing. Only now, the building was packed from wall to wall. God was moving, and nobody wanted to leave. It was 2:30 in the afternoon by the time we left that building, and I was walking on air.

What a difference a few hours make! What had started out as one of those challenging, defeating days had turned into a blessing I will never forget. I also learned the importance of being ready at all times, because God's ability to bless is not limited to the situation or the circumstances in which you find yourself.

Do you ever run up against barriers in life that seem to defeat you, or at least turn you back from your goal? Do you ever wonder why you set out in the first place?

The first thing I learned that morning is that *a big part of our training is learning to act on what God is telling us.* Life is full of challenge. But God wants us to keep moving in obedience to His voice.

Second, I found that *when we press on, a great work of God will be accomplished in us—maybe even greater than what He accomplishes through us.*

There Is No Victory Without a Fight

Christians often talk about "living in victory." That's something we'd all like to do. But the very word victory implies that a battle has been fought, that one side has emerged as the winner. There cannot be a victory unless there has been a contest or a fight of some kind. As a Christian, you may find yourself in many fights and struggles that you did not seek nor want, but when it happens, you should fight on, knowing that God is able to give you the victory.

When New Missions first went to the Haitian community of Ti Riviere, the people there gave us some land and asked us to start a school. We cleared the land, we constructed buildings, and soon we were educating and feeding more than 500 children.

We had already been doing this for ten years when one of the villagers came to us, claimed that we had built the school on his property, and demanded that we start paying him rent.

When we refused, he padlocked the buildings.

You can imagine how we felt, and how the children felt, coming in the morning and finding that their school had been closed down.

The whole community was in an uproar over this matter. In order to help settle the issue, a court in Haiti ordered someone to be sent to Ti Riviere to survey the land. What we didn't know was that the government of Haiti owns all land that is within 200 feet of the beach. When the surveyor discovered that our school was within 200 feet of the ocean, the matter was closed. We were educating and feeding our students on land that belonged to the government. The individual had no claim against us.

We had a tremendous celebration to celebrate that victory. In a way, we were thankful for the fight, because it was a validation to us of God's blessings upon our ministry.

A similar thing happened to a friend of mine named David Demola. David is the pastor of Faith Fellowship Ministries in Edison, New Jersey. He bought a piece of land at the intersection of the New Jersey Turnpike and the Garden State Parkway, where he and his congregation planned to build a huge new church.

But then the city fathers voted unanimously not to let him build there.

Four years went by while he appealed to a higher court, spending nearly $400,000 in attorney's fees in the process.

Finally, the ruling came down that the building being planned was a regional church and as such, the city had no right to stop the construction.

Soon after, Faith Fellowship Ministries began pouring the foundation for the largest church complex in the state of New Jersey. Even those who once opposed David Demola are now anxious to support him, offering to help in any way they possibly can.

He has won a tremendous victory. And like many before him, he has been strengthened by the fight!

Listening to God's Voice

Peter and the others had an advantage over you and me, no question. There was no way they could dispute what the Lord had said to them. It's a rare occasion when you or I will have an easy time discerning the Lord's will for our lives. I don't know about you, but the Lord has never spoken to me in an audible voice, and I doubt He ever will—this side of heaven.

Because we don't hear His voice that clearly, it's easy for us to become confused. But learning to hear Him is an important piece of the work God does *in* us. Because when we sense His guidance we become strong, and resolute. We are less likely to quit or be defeated.

We must learn to distinguish our own voice and dreams from those of God. Why? Because we often confuse our own desires for God's will. And our desires—unless they have been surrendered to Him—do not necessarily reflect God's will. I know of a man who felt that God was telling him to divorce his wife of thirty years and marry a younger woman. Obviously, he wasn't really listening to God, and he brought grief into a number of lives as a result.

We also need to hear God's voice because there is something in most of us that is ready to quit when things get tough. It's something that says we should not be doing what God wants us to do after all. But just because you're struggling doesn't mean that you're not following the leading of God. *His desire for you, right now, might be to strengthen you and purify your faith by taking you through a time of struggle.* In Hebrews we read that most of the heroes of faith endured difficulties in their lives. And yet many of them saw tremendous victories from God's hand *because* their faithfulness and endurance purified their faith. This brings me to my next point.

We need to stay carefully tuned to God's voice because we can deceive ourselves. We can think that because we *seem* to be enjoying God's blessings, we're living in obedience. But financial success, or any other success in life, is not a sure sign that you are living in obedience to God's will.

This leads us to the obvious question: How can you learn to hear God's voice, and, by hearing His voice, be ready to handle the opportunities and challenges He wants to give you?

I believe that wherever you are in life, you can hear God's voice in specific ways:

- In your circumstances.
- Through your Christian friends and relationships.
- Through God's Word.

God Speaks Through Your Circumstances

If you're wondering what God wants you to do with your life, here are some important questions to ask yourself:

What kind of training and education do I have?

What are my skills and strengths? (If you're not sure, ask your closest friends, including your spouse, to give you their honest assessment.)

What is the one thing in life I enjoy the most?

What is the one thing in life I like the least?

Given my training, natural skills and inclinations, what could be a likely area of service for me?

I'm not suggesting that you're going to find God's plan for your life by taking a skills assessment test. But because it is unlikely that God expects you to take a quantum leap into an area of life that is totally foreign to you, it is quite possible that you can hear Him speaking to you through your present circumstances.

When Jesus met Peter and the others, they were fishermen. That was the circumstance of their lives. God spoke to them in the middle of those circumstances. First of all, Jesus told them to use the skills they knew to catch more fish. Then He told them that, from then on, they would be fishers of men. It would have made no sense to them if He had told them to go now and harvest their crops and He would bless them, because they were fishermen, not farmers. Such language would have been foreign to the language of their souls and the understanding of life their own circumstances had formed in them.

Have you really grasped the fact that God is sovereign enough to create the very circumstances of your life? That He is using those circumstances to mold and direct you? As the Apostle Paul says in Acts 17:28, "In Him we live and move and have our being."

God Speaks to You Through Your Friends

This may seem like a bit of a contradiction. I've told you that when we first went to Haiti, quite a few people shook their heads in wonder and suggested that we had spent too much time in the tropical sun. But most of them were not close friends. The majority of those who took the time to pray with us, to hear our reasons for what we were doing, and to seek the Lord on our behalf, ended up giving us their blessing and support. There was not total agreement, but the majority agreed that we were doing what the Lord wanted us to do.

The Bible is right when it says, "For lack of guidance a nation falls, but many advisors make victory sure" (Proverbs 11:14).

I want to make it clear that when I say God can speak to you through your friends, I am talking about Christian friends. And if you don't have any Christian friends, you need to be involved in a strong church where you can have fellowship with other believers. Numbered among those Christian friends who should be listened to, I would include pastors, elders, teachers and others in positions of authority within the church.

God Speaks Through His Word

This one is simple enough, but I'm continuously surprised by how many well-meaning Christians don't know it. I mentioned earlier the man who felt God was telling him to divorce his wife. I realize that's pretty extreme. Anyone who knows the Scriptures at all knows that God is not a big fan of divorce. And anyone who knows anything of God's nature knows that it's never His desire to see a family pulled apart. But there are some other areas that are pretty fuzzy. However, if you really know God's Word, you'll have a good basis from which to begin to handle those "tricky" decisions.

Earlier, we talked about a woman named Ann who, at 57 years of age, wondered if she really ought to step out in faith and start a new career as a mentor of younger women, or if she should spend her golden years traveling and taking it easy. Well God's not against taking some time for rest and recreation. But there is no way He wants us to spend all of our time taking it easy when we have gifts that could be used to benefit others. When Paul wrote to Titus, he said, "…teach the older women to be reverent in the way they live…to teach what is good. Then they can train the younger women…." (Titus 2:3-4). I am not saying this is a personal word for Ann, but it is an illustration from God's Word regarding what He would expect from a woman like her. The Bible contains many references to the importance of believers teaching, strengthening and encouraging one another. Should Ann forget all about becoming a teacher and spend all of her time traveling? Of course not.

As you become accustomed to hearing God's voice, His Spirit is better able to help you overcome one of our last major challenges. That is, to do His will when it seems at odds with the part of our nature that wants to give up and give in to what's easy and comforting. Do you feel confident you are doing what God wants you to do? Then don't quit! Keep at it.

As Paul said: "Let us not become weary in doing good, because at the proper time we will reap a harvest if we do not give up" (Galatians 6:9).

One part of that harvest is the blessing of mature character, born out of diligence and faithfulness.

Hearing God As We Work

Americans once believed that hard work paid off. Some will tell you that this country was built on the backs of those who believed in the "Protestant Work Ethic." I still believe in it. I believe "hard work pays off" is one of the laws of the universe. If you want to have a blessing, begin to work, even if it means working all through the night. God will meet you to bless you.

I think of another man who continued to follow God when the odds were against him, and as a result, made a tremendous impact on his home village in Haiti. His story inspires me.

About eleven years ago, when New Missions was still relatively new in Haiti, my brother Timothy and my father got in a motorboat and made their way along the shoreline until they came to a little village they had not visited before.

Ti Riviere was very poor, as most rural Haitian villages are, with no clinic, no church and no school. The children there had no hope of a better life. They would grow up to be subsistence farmers and fishermen, like their parents, barely eking out a living.

But there was one man living in that village who wanted things to be different for those kids. He was a self-educated man. And he was a Christian who felt that God had called him to do what he could for the children. Because of that, he had started a small, makeshift school. Every day, he met with about fifty children in a clearing under some coconut palms, and taught reading, writing and arithmetic. He wasn't getting paid. He didn't get much in the way of appreciation. I'm sure there where times when he felt like giving up. He may have wondered how these students were going to benefit from the education he was giving them.

What difference did it make if they knew how to read and write? But in spite of the pessimism that sometimes gnawed at him, he knew that there could be no possibility of a better life without education. Besides, he was not about to turn his back on his calling, so day after day, he met with his students under the shade of those coconut trees. He gently answered their questions. He corrected their mistakes. He encouraged them to learn for the sake of learning, and to strive to better themselves.

My father and brother observed him in action the day they came ashore, and knew right away that we needed to start a school in the village. After all, we already had a teacher.

So we went to work:

- We built a school building.
- We provided school books and other materials for the children.
- We helped to organize a curriculum to ensure that the students were getting the best possible education.

And all of this happened because of one Christian who was washing and mending his nets, persevering in what he believed God wanted him to do.

Shortly after we began our work in Ti Riviere, another missionary and I rode a motorcycle out to the village, took photographs of fifty-seven children who lived there, and registered them for school. Within the next few weeks, we gave the photographs to another organization, which had indicated an interest in sponsoring all of these boys and girls.

(Every child who attends one of our schools has an outside sponsor who contributes $24 each month toward that child's expenses. New Missions in Haiti uses that money for things like textbooks, school uniforms, food, medical care and school salaries.)

For a year, we heard nothing further from this organization. Meanwhile, the kids were in school. We were feeding them, giving them health care, and teaching them about the love of Jesus, with the result that they were growing stronger in body, mind and spirit. The entire village was changing for the better. The spirit of hope we were planting in the children was affecting the parents as well. They were excited about their children becoming truly educated, getting the opportunity for a better life than they had ever known.

Finally, the other organization informed us with regret that they had decided against taking on sponsorship of the children. I told them that I was sorry about their decision, but that I understood, and would appreciate it if they would return the photos.

They couldn't find them. They spent more than a week looking for them, but they were nowhere to be found, which meant we had to start over from scratch, as far as our sponsorship efforts were concerned. I got on my motorcycle, rode back out to Ti Riviere and took photos of all the children again.

Not long after this, my parents were on the way to Cayes one afternoon when they stopped at a little soda stand for a drink. While they were there, a car filled with other Americans pulled up alongside them. Now if you're an American in Haiti, and you see another American, you're just naturally going to strike up a conversation with them, which is exactly what my parents did. They discovered that the visitors were Christians who had come to Haiti on a short missions trip. The leader of the group was looking for missions to visit and asked my father if they could see New Missions. My father invited them to come to our compound for dinner on Saturday night.

To this day, my mother will admit that she wasn't thrilled by my father's generosity. Saturday was supposed to be her day off, and now she would be cooking dinner for fifteen people, including our own family. But nevertheless, Mom smiled and said that, sure, she'd love to have them, and she cooked an Italian dinner.

My parents especially enjoyed talking to two of the visitors, a businessman from California named Jim Loomis, and Harry Thomas, who was a pastor from New Jersey. At one point in the conversation, my dad mentioned our work in Ti Riviere.

Jim was thoughtful for a moment and then asked, "How many children are there?"

"Fifty-seven," my dad replied.

Jim's eyes opened wide.

"Did you say...*fifty*-seven?"

"That's right."

A smile split Jim's face from ear to ear.

"Well, that explains why I'm here," he said.

He went on to say that a year earlier, he was on an airplane between Dallas and Los Angeles, and he had been praying that God would give him some direction for his life.

He related to my parents that after he had prayed that prayer, "A quiet voice kept coming to me saying, 'Go to Haiti' and 'fifty children.'" Who these children were or what he was supposed to do for them, he didn't know.

But because he wanted to be obedient to God's voice, he had scheduled back to back two one-week trips to Haiti with different organizations. It was on the second trip that he met my parents, and agreed to have dinner with them a few nights before he was due to return to the United States.

He remembers now that when the night of the scheduled dinner arrived, he and his companions didn't want to go because they were so tired. Jim was also feeling frustrated because, after two weeks in Haiti, he still had no clear picture of what God wanted him to do. But despite his fatigue and frustration, Jim and his friends finally decided for some reason that they should keep their dinner engagement.

As Jim recalls, when he heard about the children in Ti Riviere, "A chill went down my back as I realized this was the reason God had sent me to Haiti."

He told my parents that as soon as he got home, he was going to talk to the Missions pastor of his church about sponsoring all of those children.

And that's exactly what he did.

I think that story would be amazing if it ended there. It says something wonderful about God's love for children everywhere. It thrills me to think that He would speak to the heart of a businessman from California and bring him all the way to Haiti to care for fifty hopeless, helpless children. Jim sponsored all fifty-seven children himself until he could find other sponsors for them.

It says something about that teacher, who kept at it day after day, in spite of the fact that he had no classrooms, no textbooks or books of any kind, in fact, and no paper, no pens, no pencils, nothing. But he kept on keeping on because he felt certain that he was doing what God had called him to do.

After Jim went back to California, I got a call from the organization that had originally been interested in sponsoring the children. No, they hadn't changed their minds, but they had found the photos, and were sending them back to me. When I got them, I was amazed at the difference that had taken place in the children between the first and second set of photographs I took.

In the first set of photos, most of the children were dressed in rags. They were emaciated, their eyes were dull, and their shoulders were slouched, showing their lack of confidence and purpose in life. In the second set photographed a year later, they stood tall and proud in their new school uniforms. They looked healthy, their eyes sparkled. Not only that, but during my second visit to the village, I was able to photograph the children standing in front of the school building we had constructed.

I was feeling pretty good about everything, until I got a call from the missions pastor of Jim's church. He was gracious and polite, but wanted me to know that the church's missions budget for the coming year was totally accounted for. There was no way they could add the sponsorship of fifty-seven children.

He did agree, though, that he would take the matter before the entire congregation, and that I could send him the children's photos. Well, of course, I did more than send the fifty-seven photos. I sent both sets of photos, because I wanted to show as clearly as possible the difference that sponsorship was making in the lives of those kids. Meanwhile, Jim was hard at work, actively seeking sponsors for the children.

When the members of that church saw those kids' photos, there was no question about sponsoring them. The answer was a resounding, "Yes," as individual members of the congregation decided that they wanted to be involved in our work in Ti Riviere.

Not only were all fifty-seven children sponsored, but the church wanted to know if we had any more boys and girls in that village who needed help.

Jim says, "As the time went by our Missions Committee began sending teams to Haiti and the pastors themselves were touched and brought Haiti back to Southern California. Our church has never been the same. George and Jeanne [DeTellis] began visiting our church and church members were able to get a realistic picture of another culture that they could impact and that could impact them and their children."

He adds that, "South Coast Community Church and I have been touched and changed in a most wonderful way. My vision is for this same wonderful relationship that has been wrought by God to continue in an ever-increasing way, both with South Coast and other churches. It is true that the 'giver' gets more than the 'receiver.'"

Remember—When God Moves He *Moves*!

Isn't it amazing how God works? I believe it was for the sake of those fifty-seven children that He caused the first organization to misplace the children's photos, that He kept us hanging on for a year, that He had me go to the trouble of riding back to the village to photograph those children a second time. He did all of that because He wanted to ensure that all of those children received the best possible care over the long-term. I believe it was part of God's plan for my parents to stop into that little soda stand for a drink, and that my father would invite the Americans to dinner on a Saturday night. There is not a detail that escapes God's attention. I don't pretend to know how He does it. I just know that He does.

There were many times along the way when we were discouraged about what would happen to those kids. We felt as if we had worked all night long, and had nothing to show for it.

But in the end, God was faithful. And now, all we can do is praise Him!

—⁓— —⁓— —⁓—

Nothing you ever do when you are committed to God will be wasted or go unrewarded. When you give all your strength and effort to Him, He will honor you. He will create new strength and confidence in you, such as you have never known before.

Six

Risky Living

*"For whoever wants to save his life will lose it, but
whoever loses his life for me will save it."*
— Luke 9:24

*W*hat was a nice Pentecostal boy like me doing in a
church like this? I knew it was a risk right from the start.
On this particular occasion I had accepted a speaking engagement at a small Baptist church in upstate New York. I knew before
I accepted that this church had a reputation of not being open
toward those of us whose religious practice tended to be more
"expressive." But I have to take risks, for the sake of the Haitian
children who need to see a tangible expression of God's love.

And despite my initial misgivings, my talk went well. The members of the congregation were genuinely interested in doing what
they could to take the love of Jesus to poor children in Haiti, and
even though I'll admit to being a trifle nervous, I felt very welcome.

And then came the reception after the service. That's when
he zeroed in on me.

I saw him coming from all the way across the crowded fellowship hall. He was probably in his eighties, wearing a black suit,
with a huge mop of white hair, and he was headed straight for me.
When he got within about ten feet, I saw that he was carrying a

massive Bible under one arm. The thing must have weighed fifteen pounds. On the front of his black Bible, big gold letters read "King James Giant Print Version."

I breathed a silent prayer of protection. "Oh, Lord, this guy realizes that I'm a Pentecostal, and he's coming over here to whip me. Please, Lord. Help me to...."

Too late. He was practically nose to nose with me.

"I want to talk to you," he announced. He sounded an awful lot like Charlton Heston in *The Ten Commandments*.

"Great," I responded, suddenly aware that my own voice wasn't as deep and dramatic as I'd like it to be. "Last Sunday night I heard a TV evangelist preach a message on television that speaking in tongues is of the devil. What do you think about that?" he asked.

I opened my mouth, praying that God would put some wisdom in there.

"Well, I was born and raised a Pentecostal," I began. "My grandparents were Pentecostals; it's all I've ever known. I don't know about the TV evangelist's sermon, but I'll tell you this, if I was born and raised a Baptist, I would be a *good* Baptist."

The old gentleman lit up like a Christmas tree. He threw his head back and laughed.

"Yup!" he said. "I'll bet you would."

He reached out for my hand, pumped it like I was some long-lost friend, and then disappeared into the crowd.

Thank you, Lord!

I was delighted that I had been willing to risk coming and speak there, not only because of the chance it gave me to talk about our work in Haiti but because I felt, in some small way, God had used me to build a bridge across denominational and doctrinal boundaries.

Now that may seem like a small risk to you but it was not to me. Speaking in a church that is not friendly to my tradition can be a real challenge and a risk. But it's something I have to do, because it is something God calls me to do to see His work in Haiti succeed.

Simply put, if you want to accomplish great things in your life, you must be willing to take risks. You must be willing to risk falling down, willing to risk making mistakes as you learn, willing to risk losing, willing to risk looking like a fool, and willing to risk the wrath and scorn of those who don't care to understand why you're doing what you're doing.

When the disciples got back in that boat and headed back out on the lake at Jesus' command, they were taking a big risk.

I wonder if there were other fishermen on the lakeshore that day who were watching the disciples. If they were, I can imagine them nudging each other with their elbows.

"What are those guys doing?"

"Can you believe it? They've been out there all night, and now, because this guy thinks they can catch some fish, they're going to row all the way back out there?"

"What? They're going to risk getting their nets all wet, and dirty, and torn for nothing?"

"That's right!"

"Oh, this I gotta see!"

If the disciples hadn't caught any fish that day, they would have looked like fools to the other members of their profession.

But because they were willing to take that risk, they caught more fish than their boat could hold, and they received the calling that would change their lives for all eternity.

Do you remember the four people we talked about earlier? There was Joey, the college student; Sally, the housewife; Ben, the middle-aged repairman; and Ann, the grandmother. All of them had dreams and ambitions that lay beyond what they were doing at present. All of them had the skills and abilities they needed to achieve those dreams. But not one of them would have ever made it without a willingness to take risks.

Risk-Takers Who Made It

Frank Peretti's *This Present Darkness* has sold hundreds of thousands of copies, and is one of the best-selling Christian novels of all time. And yet for the longest time nobody seemed to be interested. No publisher wanted to take a chance. Christians, they said, didn't want to read novels, even if they are well-crafted and exciting.

But Peretti refused to listen. He persisted until his novel found a home and *This Present Darkness,* along with his subsequent novels, has impacted thousands of lives for Christ.

When a young Elvis Presley entered a talent show in Nashville, he was practically booed off the stage, and urged not to give up his job as a truck driver. But Elvis had dreams that were much bigger than driving a truck, and the rest is history.

Very few people make it to the top in any area of life without a willingness to take risks.

When my family went to Haiti, we took risks. My dad resigned the pastorate of a growing, established church to begin a ministry in one of the world's poorest, most primitive countries. To understand the type of risk he was taking, you'd have to know how long and hard my father worked to build that church in New England. He had gone through some very lean years there, and now, just when he had reached the point where he could feel more secure, where he could command a salary that would allow him to have the little extras he had always denied himself, he quit and left for Haiti.

There were quite a few people who talked to him as if he must be crazy to give up the secure life to go off to the jungles of Haiti. But it was a risk he knew he had to take. There were also many times after the work was begun in Haiti when we had to accept risks to stay there. Since New Missions has been working in Haiti, the country has been through nine governments, a United Nations embargo, a United Nations intervention and two economic embargoes. We stayed in Haiti through the invasion of 24,000 American troops, and the ensuing dangers that invasion brought with it. We have maintained our ministry in the face of two economic blockades that only compounded the misery and poverty in Haiti, and made our work much harder than ever before. Three times the American Embassy requested that we leave the island and, in fact, offering to help us evacuate.

At any point along the way, my father, and the rest of the family, could have given up and said, "This is too risky. Let's go home and let someone else handle things from now on." But my family hung in there, and because we were willing to take that risk, thousands of Haitian children are being educated, fed and provided for, and thousands of souls have come into God's kingdom.

Where Risk Is Necessary

If you desire to be all God wants you to be, there are several areas of life where risk is required.

1) You must be willing to take risks in interpersonal relationships.

Pastor-author John Maxwell tells a story about an event that happened when he was a young man, just twenty-five years old, fresh out of seminary. A friend, who was the pastor of a large church, came to John and said he was thinking seriously about resigning his position. It seems there was one man in the church named Jim, the chairman of the lay leadership board, who opposed him at every turn, and he simply could not take it any longer.

Maxwell urged his friend to hang in there, but the man had simply had enough. Within the week, he turned in his resignation. Not long after that, the church's governing board called Maxwell and offered him the position. Now you might think that after all he had heard from his friend, the last thing John Maxwell would have done was to accept the pastorate of that church, but he felt that God was leading him to take the job.

A few days after he had accepted the position, but before he had officially begun serving as pastor, Maxwell quietly slipped into the balcony to watch as a congregational business meeting took place in the auditorium below. It was more like a war than a meeting, and it raged for four hours. The conflict centered on whether the church should build a new activity center. Jim was leading the opposition, and he was not about to be moved. Threats and counter-threats flew back and forth among the 500 or so who were present that evening, and for a while it appeared likely that the church was going to split over the issue. I imagine that as John Maxwell watched that meeting from the safety of the balcony, he began to wonder if he should reconsider accepting the church's job offer.

But he also knew the potential the church had for saving souls and reaching its community with Christ's love. That was why he had taken the risk of accepting the pastorate in the first place.

A few days later, during his first day on the job as pastor of that church, John decided to take an even bigger risk. He called Jim and asked him to come in for a meeting. And then, when Jim arrived, Maxwell sat down with him and mapped out his vision for the church's future. He told Jim that he valued his opinion and, because Jim was in his late sixties, his wisdom born of experience. For that reason, Maxwell asked for a weekly meeting where they could discuss church concerns.

Finally, he said, "Now, I've had people tell me that you're hard to get along with. In fact, I've heard you're a troublemaker."

Before the man could protest, John continued, "This is what I've heard, but I have no way of knowing if it's true. This is my first day on the job, and we have a brand new slate in front of us."

"Now, suppose you have ten years left, and then God calls you home? What are you going to say when He asks you about your life? You can tell him that this green kid came along, and that you fought with him, and that he won some and you won some. That there were a lot of battles and the congregation just drifted along. Or you can tell him that this young kid came along, and you took him under your wing and helped him and that the two of you did great things together, and that those were the best ten years this church ever knew. What is it going to be?"

Jim didn't say anything. Instead, he pushed his chair back, got up and walked out of Maxwell's office, with the young pastor right behind him. Maxwell followed him to a drinking fountain in the hall, where Jim stooped over for a drink. Maxwell remembers that the man drank, drank and drank some more for more than a minute while he stood there watching, wondering what he was going to do and say when he was finished.

Finally, Jim lifted his face from the fountain, and when he did, Maxwell saw that it was covered with tears.

Jim wrapped the young preacher in a bear hug and said, "I'll be in your corner."

John Maxwell pastored that church for the next eight and one-half years, and he remembers it now as a time of wonderful accomplishments for God's kingdom. As for Jim, Maxwell now says, "He became my number one ally." They were able to do great things together.

But what would have happened if John hadn't taken the risk of confronting that gentleman? Chances are very good that in a few years, Maxwell would have left that pulpit himself, rubbing his hands together and saying, "good riddance," as he did. But because he was willing to take a risk in the matter of a personal relationship, what could have been a time of trouble and loss was turned into a personal victory.

Not every personal confrontation will go as well as the one John Maxwell reported, but the point is that you have to be willing to take the risk.

2) You must be willing to risk getting yourself into a situation from which you cannot retreat.

I am afraid that many of us are willing to trust God only so far. We're like bungee jumpers. We're only willing to take a leap of faith if we're sure we have cords tied around our waist that will keep us from hitting the ground, in case God doesn't catch us.

But you're hardly taking a risk at all if you're only willing to go out far enough that you can make it safely back to shore if you should get into trouble.

Almost everyone knows the Bible story of the time when Jesus came to His disciples by walking on the water. We all know that Peter asked the Lord if he could walk on the water also, and that the Lord said, "Come," and that, for a few brief moments, Peter was dancing along on the top of the waves as if they were made out of linoleum or something solid. But then he took his eyes off the Lord, began to be fearful, and immediately started to sink.

For nearly 2,000 years, that story has been told to demonstrate Peter's lack of faith. But I think people who see it that way are missing the point. *Peter is the only one who got out of the boat to try to walk on the water!* The other disciples sat there, looking at each other and thinking, "Man, he's got to be crazy to try that." Yes, it was a lack of faith that caused Peter to begin to sink, but it was courage that caused him to get out there on the water to begin with. And I think we ought to learn at least as much from Peter's willingness to take a risk.

I recently read a fascinating book entitled, *The Art of War,* which was written in China in 500 B.C. Sun Tzu, the author, believed that one of the strategies for winning decisively on the battlefield is to thrust the troops into a life-or-death situation, from which there is no possible retreat. Sun Tzu did not see it as a disadvantage to have troops backed up against the walls of a sheer cliff, for example, because it meant they would fight that much harder. If it got to the point where they were no longer fighting for their king or their country, but for their very lives, they would fight with a skill and a ferocity that often led to tremendous victory.

I think this has a practical application to the life of every Christian. It is only when you are willing to get yourself into the position where you know you can't quit, that you will have your greatest success.

3) Be willing to let go of what's in your hand so you can take hold of something new.

Are you willing to let go of what you're holding onto today, for the sake of what God wants to give you tomorrow?

Please understand that I am not talking about behaving foolishly, nor about taking unnecessary risks. But I am talking about being willing to follow the Lord's calling on your life, even if it means risking everything you have worked your entire life to gain.

As an example, I think of my decision to move New Missions from the Boston area to Orlando. I felt certain that God was calling us to Orlando, because of its strategic location, and its development as a world media center. But it was not at all easy to risk losing what we had all worked hard for so long to build in New England.

On the personal level, we were living in a big, old Victorian house with three stories and plenty of room. We had lived in that house for ten years. It was home to me, and I hated to leave it. If I could have, I would have put it on a trailer and moved it to Florida with me. I loved that house and had just remodeled the entire place. I had refinished the banisters and all the hardwood floors. It was a beautiful, beautiful house, but because the Lord said "Go," I walked away from it. Not only that, but I did it during the bottom of the real estate bust in New England, which means I sold that beautiful house for half of what it is worth today.

Nevertheless, I knew beyond any doubt that we were doing what the Lord wanted us to do, and He has poured out His blessing on our ministry because of it. What's more, after we made the move to Orlando, He confirmed in a most exciting way that we had done the right thing.

What happened was this: In September of 1992, I made a visit to Orlando to begin laying the groundwork for our move. Because I didn't know anyone there, I opened the yellow pages and randomly picked out a real estate broker. When I went to her office, I was happy to find out that she was a Christian, and active in a local church. But despite that pleasant surprise, most of the day was discouraging. I didn't see any rentals that appealed to me.

Toward the end of the day, she took me to an empty lot in a nice neighborhood where one of her clients was planning to build a rental house. She could show me another house like the one he would build here, but this one wouldn't be ready until January. She thought that might be a problem for me, but actually, I took it as a simple sign that God was with us in the move. The truth was, we weren't moving to Florida until after the first of the year. What she was proposing was perfect. I agreed to rent the house-to-be.

In January we moved to Orlando, into a brand-new house. If you've been through a winter in New England, you can imagine how excited my wife Paula and I were to be moving to Florida in the middle of January. It was warm and sunny. The grass was green. People were playing golf. Lakes and ponds were alive with ducks and geese. It was wonderful.

It was also wonderful to be moving into a brand-new house in a brand-new community!

We were still unloading boxes when the woman who lived across the street came over to say hello.

"Hi," she said, "My name is Denise. I just wanted to welcome you to the neighborhood." She told us that she thought we were going to like it here and said to let her know if we needed to use the phone or anything.

In the course of our conversation, she told us that she and her husband had only been living in the neighborhood for about a month.

"I saw your license plate," she said, "and I noticed that you're from Massachusetts. You'll have to meet my husband, because he's from Massachusetts, too."

"Really? What part?"

"Worcester."

I tapped my chest with my forefinger. "*I'm* from Worcester," I said. "What's your husband's name? Maybe I know him."

She shook her head and laughed. "I doubt that. Our last name is Smith."

"Well, what's your husband's first name?"

"Curt."

I almost shouted it. "I know Curt Smith! We're the DeTellis's."

Her mouth dropped open and she stared at me for what seemed like five minutes. Finally she said, "I've heard a lot about you… This is just incredible."

Curt Smith had been an elder in my father's church in Worcester. Not only that, but he had been one of the first to catch our vision for Haiti, and had spent 18 months there as a missionary.

After that, he had gone to Florida to attend college and get his engineering degree. He had met Denise in Florida, married her, and now here we were, literally next-door neighbors. Curt Smith is a terrific man of God, someone with an encouraging, edifying spirit. It was comforting to know that God, in His wisdom and mercy, had made it possible for me to renew my acquaintance with this old friend, and that He had also placed me in the position of benefiting from his encouraging spirit and wise counsel.

Knowing that God had arranged it so the two of us were going to live right across the street from each other sent goosebumps up and down my spine.

I hadn't seen Curt Smith in five years, and it had been at least a year and a half since I had even talked to him. I had called him when I first began thinking that the Lord was leading us to relocate to central Florida. After that, I'd lost touch with him. I had no idea where he was or what he was doing. But the Lord knew.

When I got over my initial shock, I said to his wife, "Don't tell him about this. We've got to surprise him. Bring him over tonight to meet the new neighbors, and let's see what happens."

When Curt rang the bell that evening, I rushed to open it, and it was as if someone had plugged us both into an electric socket! That feeling lasted for weeks. It was so strange to look out my window and see my old friend working in his yard. It was a sign to me that God had us both exactly where He wanted us to be. He didn't leave us to second-guess the risky step we'd taken. He wanted us to know we'd done the right thing by giving up our life in New England for a new life in Florida.

4) Be willing to risk mistakes and failures in order to grow.

Most of us have an inordinate fear of failure. Why? Is it pride? I tend to think it's just the opposite. We fear failure because we have low self-esteem. We're afraid that if we fail, other people will find out how weak and/or inept we are. Some people even confuse low self-esteem with Christian humility, but the two things really have nothing at all to do with each other.

It is relatively easy to risk failure, and to endure it when it comes, if you understand the success that is ultimately yours in Christ.

You can risk failure when you understand that you are a unique part of God's creation, a human being made in God's own image.

You can risk failure when you understand that you have your own unique gifts, which were given to you to enable you to fulfill the destiny that God has planned for you.

You can risk failure when you realize that occasional setbacks or failures are insignificant in the long run. They are insignificant because you are an integral part of something greater than yourself, something God has planned to do in and through you.

5) Be willing to risk facing your own true soul.

Do you know what you believe? Do you know why you believe it? What I am talking about here is stepping right up to the edge of your faith and discovering its true content.

Think for a moment about what the disciples were doing when, at Jesus' word, they got back in the boat and sailed out on the lake to fish. They had to reload their nets, get back in the boat and launch out all at the least likely time of day to catch fish: morning, when the sun was coming up, the fish had been feeding all night, and were now headed for the bottom to rest again. But they did it because they believed Jesus when He told them they would catch fish. They were really putting their faith on the line. If they hadn't caught any fish, it would have showed them that their faith in Jesus was misplaced. They would have been left thinking, "Boy, that guy sure made a great speech, but when we tried to put the things he said into practice, there just wasn't anything there." But, you see, there *is* something there. Only when you step out in faith will you discover that the Gospel is solid, real, a thing of substance.

What You Get When You're Willing to Risk

When you are willing to take risks like the ones we've been discussing, you get some very important dividends. People who are willing to risk:

- Find out who they are.
- Discover the weak parts, as well as the strong parts, of their character and faith.
- Enter into the path that will carry them to their destiny, and an understanding that a few missteps or failures along the way won't defeat them.
- Begin to grow, as human beings, mature adults and Christians.

—ᴡᴡ—   —ᴡᴡ—   —ᴡᴡ—

People who are willing to risk are the ones most likely to meet their destiny and find fulfillment, not the ones who sit safely on the steady shores of life.

Seven

The "Nevertheless" Principle

Master, we have toiled all night and caught nothing;
nevertheless at Your Word I will let down the net.
—Luke 5:5 NKJV

Six-year-old Dieuvil, who lived in the Haitian village of LaSalle, desperately wanted to go to school. He would hang around, watching through the coconut thatch classrooms while the other children were in school, and sometimes he'd come in and help our teacher serve them lunch.

He wanted more than anything to learn, to be like the other kids. But he wasn't like them. He couldn't speak. And in Haiti, if a child is deaf, dumb, or blind, he is often the object of brutal ridicule. That was the way it was with Dieuvil. The other children laughed at him and called him "BeBe" because of the grunting sounds he made whenever he tried to talk.

Still, he came every day, and eventually won the heart of our missionary, a young woman named Kim Carroll. Even though Dieuvil wasn't sponsored, Kim asked for permission to let him eat lunch with the other children. How could we turn him away?

Soon afterward, Kim left Haiti and was replaced by another missionary named Sharon Keeler Arbough, who also fell in love with the good-natured little boy. Eventually, she asked for permission to give him a uniform and let him sit in her first-grade class. This was a more difficult request.

As far as we knew, Dieuvil might be retarded.

"Nevertheless," Sharon persisted.

We didn't even know if he was capable of learning.

Nevertheless....

Even if his mind was okay, how were we going to get through to him?

Nevertheless....

And he wasn't sponsored.

Nevertheless....

As every objection was raised, Sharon pressed us, because she loved the boy and felt sure that she could help him. Again, what could we do in the face of all that but approve her request. The boy was given a uniform, and his eyes shone bright with happiness when he realized that he was going to get a chance to go to school officially.

Sometime later, while in the village of LaSalle, my father decided to visit the school there, and was surprised to see Dieuvil sitting in the second row.

Turning to Sharon, he asked, "How is he getting along these days?"

At best, he expected to hear that the other children were more accepting of the boy now, and that he was not a disruptive influence in the classroom. He was surprised when Sharon replied, "He has the third highest grades in the class." Then she went to her desk, shuffled through some papers, and pulled out one that Dieuvil had written. The boy whom others had considered to be retarded and worthless had beautiful, elegant penmanship. His handwriting seemed to say something about what was going on inside, the person he was, deep where others could not see.

Shortly after this, Dieuvil was sponsored by a wonderful woman who wanted a "special child" to love and care for, to help guide into God's kingdom. Because of two women who were willing to say "nevertheless," this young deaf boy has received opportunities in life that otherwise would have been quite impossible for a child born in a poor Haitian village, much less for one born without the ability to speak.

Kim and Sharon were both demonstrating what you could call "The Nevertheless Principle." This principle was put into practice by the Apostle Peter during his very first encounter with Christ: He told the Lord that even though he and his friends had been out on the lake all night long without catching anything, "Nevertheless, at your word, I will let down the net." In other words, "Because *you* say so, Jesus, I'll give it another try" (Luke 5:5 NKJV).

For Peter and the others, that was the moment when patient endurance for the sake of godliness was born. It was the moment of decision, the point in time when Peter could have said, "Oh, no, bag this! I've had enough fishing for one day. I don't want to haul these heavy nets back out of the water again, especially if they're empty. I'm going to go on home and get some shuteye." If he had done that, he may have walked out of the Lord's life, out of the pages of history, and he would have lived and died as an obscure Jewish fisherman. He could have done that, but he didn't. Instead, he moved quickly in obedience to the Lord's word.

The Nevertheless Principle is about moving full speed ahead, even though:

- Circumstances seem to be stacked against you.
- You've tried before and failed.
- Others tell you it can't be done.
- You're tired and feel like giving up.
- Or, when, for any reason, discouragement wants to defeat you.

To follow The Nevertheless Principle is to act on your faith, to take that leap into the air if you have to, knowing that God will be there to support and carry you, as you act upon the direction He has given you.

My youngest brother, Tim, tells of the time he learned first-hand the importance of saying "nevertheless," and continuing when things aren't going the way you'd like them to.

Tim, who spent four years of his youth in Haiti, is an excellent musician, and in the early days of our ministry in Haiti he played the piano for dad's evangelistic services. He would load his electric piano and a little portable generator onto his Honda four-wheeler and go out to a village a couple hours before my father's arrival to get things ready. He'd put up some lights, a speaker, and get everything set up for the service. When dad showed up, the lights were turned on, the music began to play, and a large crowd would gather.

But on one particular occasion, Tim went out to a village, got everything set up, began to crank the generator, and nothing happened. He cranked and cranked, but there was no reaction. The thing would not produce so much as a tiny spark of power.

It was getting dark by the time my father came, along with some other missionaries who were going to assist in the service. Tim walked over to them, shaking his head, told them the generator was dead, and suggested they postpone the service.

Dad shook his head. They didn't have power, or lights, or a piano. But they had the Gospel, and they wouldn't go home without sharing it with the people of this village.

By the dim light of an oil lamp, dad preached to the small crowd that gathered about the salvation that's offered through the love of Christ. At the end of his sermon, he called for those who wanted to surrender their lives to Christ to step forward. Nobody came.

He gave a second altar call, speaking eloquently in Creole about the eternal love of Christ. Again, no response.

He was just about to close the service, when a lone figure stepped out of the darkness and into the small circle of light shed by the oil lamp. The Gospel had found its mark in the heart of a painfully shy nine-year-old girl. And now, with tears in her eyes, she had come forward to publicly surrender her life to Christ.

Tim watched as our dad prayed with that little girl, and he knew beyond any doubt that she was the one for whom God had sent them to that little village. She was the one for whom my father said, in essence, "We may not have electricity, nevertheless, Lord, at Your word, we will stay and preach the Gospel."

As Tim listened to that child ask Jesus into her heart, his mind turned to the parable of the lost sheep, Jesus' story about the Good Shepherd, who left the ninety-nine sheep that were safely in the fold to go in search of the one lamb that was lost. This little girl was Jesus' lost lamb, and He had sent our team to her village in order that they might lead her to the safety of His arms.

I May Not Like It Lord, Nevertheless...

That is the type of thing that happens when you learn to say, "nevertheless." Souls are saved. Lives are changed. Victories are won.

Watchman Nee has some excellent words that have to do with learning to say "nevertheless" to God:

Some of us know well that, in order to go on with God, we have to many a time go against the voice of the soul—our own or other people's—and to let the Cross come in to silence that appeal for self-preservation.

Am I afraid of the will of God? [A dear Christian woman who had a great] influence on the course of my life, many times asked me the question: 'Do you like the will of God?' It is a tremendous question. She did not ask, 'Do you do the will of God?' She always asked, 'Do you like the will of God?' That question goes deeper than anything else. I remember once she was having a controversy with the Lord over a certain matter. She knew what the Lord wanted, and in her heart she wanted it too. But it was difficult, and I heard her pray like this: 'Lord I confess I don't like it, but please do not give in to me. Just wait, Lord—and I will give in to thee.' She did not want the Lord to yield to her and to reduce His demands upon her. She wanted nothing but to please Him.

Many a time we have to come to the place where we are willing to let go to Him things we think to be good and precious—yes, and even, it may be, the very things of God themselves—that his will may be done."[5]

There is the principle in action: I may not like your will, Lord, nevertheless, because I am committed to following you, I am also committed to obeying your will. And, Lord, help me learn to like it.

The greatest example occurred in the Garden of Gethsemane. Jesus, prior to His arrest, fell prostrate on the ground and prayed, "My Father, if it is possible, may this cup be taken from me. Yet not as I will, but as you will" (Matthew 26:39). That was a time of agony for Christ, as He contemplated betrayal at the hands of Judas, abandonment by His friends, and the physical and spiritual pain He would have to endure during His hours on the cross. Nevertheless, Jesus was willing to obey His Father's will. And because He was obedient, every man, woman and child on this planet has access to abundant, eternal life.

That was not the first time Jesus had demonstrated His allegiance to this principle. In fact, He unerringly followed The Nevertheless Principle many times during His earthly ministry.

Matthew 16 contains an account of what happened when Jesus first began telling His disciples that He was going to suffer and die for the sins of the world:

"Peter took him aside and began to rebuke him. 'Never, Lord!' he said. 'This shall never happen to you!'

"Jesus turned and said to Peter, 'Get behind me, Satan! You are a stumbling block to me; you do not have in mind the things of God, but the things of men.'"

In effect, Jesus was saying, "I know this isn't what *you* want for me, Peter. And I am certainly not looking forward to going through it myself. Nevertheless, I came into the world to suffer and die for the sins of mankind, and that is exactly what I am going to do."

In Luke 13, we find this story:

"At that time some Pharisees came to Jesus and said to him, 'Leave this place and go somewhere else. Herod wants to kill you.'

"He replied, 'Go tell that fox, "I will drive out demons and heal people today and tomorrow, and on the third day I will reach my goal." In any case, I must keep going today and tomorrow and the next day—for surely no prophet can die outside Jerusalem.'"

Jesus knew that His enemies were waiting for Him in Jerusalem. Nevertheless, He continued moving straight toward the holy city and the sorrow that awaited Him there.

All of us owe our very salvation to Christ's willingness to say "nevertheless" and keep moving toward His appointment with the cross.

The Power of a Single Word

Great power is unleashed when you are determined to follow through on your commitments, no matter who or what may try to prevent you from keeping them. There is power in the word, "nevertheless," as in, I know it doesn't look too good right now, nevertheless, I'm going to do it.

When you say "nevertheless" and move out in faith:

- Something changes in you.
- Something changes in your world.
- Something changes for the people you love.

First, *something changes in you.* You go from being a *hearer* of the word to becoming a *doer* of the word (James 1:22). You take ownership of your life. You begin to learn new responsibilities. You set out on a new path.

Remember Ben, our 43-year-old father of three who wants to do something more with his life? He wants to step out in faith, but he's thinking, "I'm 43 years old. I'm not an old man, but I'm not exactly young any more." Sometimes, he feels like a bit of a fool to even imagine that God could take an ordinary man like him and use him to do something extraordinary, especially at this point in his life.

At 43, Ben is no naïve idealist. He's taken it on the chin more than once. He's been lied to a time or two. He's been taken advantage of simply because he tried to be a good guy. And more than once he's seen all the work he's put into reaching a goal get wiped out in an instant. Like the time he saved a lot of money to take the family to Disney World, and then the transmission went out in the Chevy. It's a build-up of those "little" frustrations that has dampened his enthusiasm, caused him to be a bit fearful, and left him thinking that it's probably better just to sit tight right where he is rather than step out in faith and try to do something new.

But it doesn't matter that Ben is 43. It doesn't matter that he's had some rough times in his life. What matters is that God is calling him to greater service. If he's willing to put aside his fears and his past failures and say, nevertheless, Lord, I will do what you want me to do, there is no limit to what God will accomplish through him.

The prophet Isaiah writes that he heard the voice of the Lord saying, "Whom shall I send? And who will go for us? And I said, 'Here am I. Send me'" (Isaiah 6:8).

I believe that *right now* the eyes of the Lord are searching the earth, looking for someone He can send to do His will; someone who is willing to say, I may not be much, Lord, nevertheless, I am willing to do whatever you want me to do. Send me.

Have you ever heard it said that it's not your ability that matters as much as your *availability*? That may be a familiar cliché but there is a lot of truth in it!

As Jesus walked along the shore at the Sea of Galilee, people crowded in behind him, wanting to hear the words of wisdom that came from His lips. He looked around for the best possible platform, and His eye fell on Peter's boat. It wasn't a yacht, just a rickety little fishing boat. But it was available to Him. And Peter was available to row him out a little distance from the shore so he could stand in the boat and preach to the people gathered on the shore. Because Peter and his boat were available to the Lord, many lives were changed forever that morning, including Peter's.

When I think of the importance of being available to God, the beautiful little Haitian village of Borlance comes to mind. It is a picture-perfect little community, fronted by the whitest, most pristine beach you've ever seen, with rows of coconut palms lined up on the shoreline. A short distance away from those trees sits a cluster of little grass huts, surrounded by sugarcane fields and primitive jungle. It's a beautiful place.

When we first went there, however, there was a difficult reality beneath the picture-perfect surface. There was no church. No school. And many of the children were malnourished.

But because we were available, God sent us there to start a school, to preach the Gospel, and to help the people improve their community. Today, the beauty that strikes your eye when you first enter that little village is not an illusion. Life is good for the people of Borlance.

But a short distance up the shore, there's another village where we have not yet been able to start a work. The children there do not go to school, or church. Many of them are hungry. There's no paying work for the men so families are poorly cared for.

It may be that in that village there is one Christian family. And in that family, there is a little girl who loves Jesus with all her heart. When she goes to bed late at night after working in the fields all day, her stomach burns with hunger. And lying there in the darkness, she begins to pray, "Jesus, help my village. Help my family. Help my father find work. Please, Jesus, send someone to help us."

And I believe that in heaven, as Almighty God looks down upon her and listens to her prayer, His heart is broken. His eyes burn with compassion as He searches the earth, looking for a man or woman He can send; someone who will answer that little girl's desperate prayer.

Now, I'm not really sure where that little girl lives, but I feel that, somewhere in Haiti, she exists. And I am certain that God is looking for men and women He can use to help answer the prayers, not only of that little girl, but of all the Haitian people who are crying out to Him for help. Who will go as His representative? Who will go to tell the people of Jesus' death on the cross for their sins? Who can He send that will show them a tangible expression of His love by working with them to improve their lives? He can't send anyone who isn't willing to go. He needs someone who is available.

"I don't have much to offer you, Lord, nevertheless, I am available. Use me." That's the attitude God is looking for. When you surrender yourself to Him, He *will* use you, and you will never be the same.

Again, I'm not saying that you need to come to Haiti. I use Haiti as an example because I know it well, and because many people's lives have been changed because they obeyed God's command to go there. I have seen many people who thought they were coming for a week, or a month, because they felt God wanted them to give a little of themselves to full-time missions work. They planned to put in their time in Haiti, and then go home and resume normal life. But once they began to work among the Haitian people, their entire perspective changed. You might say their souls caught fire, and they couldn't even think of going back to their old way of life. A number of them have gone into full-time missions work, not only in Haiti, but all over the world.

On the other hand, I know of many people who have come to Haiti, not because they felt God's calling to do so, but because they were motivated by guilt. Most of those people couldn't wait to get out of Haiti and back to their comfortable routines. So again, the most important question is, "What is God calling you to do?" Whatever it is, when you begin to pursue it with your whole heart something powerful begins to take place in you. From that moment on, you are following a different path through life. It may not be an easy one, but it is sure to be fulfilling and full of opportunities for personal growth.

When the disciples made the decision to follow Jesus and become "fishers of men" they embarked upon a path that took them toward the cross and the sorrow it would bring them. And it was not only Christ's cross they would have to endure; each of them had his own personal cross to carry. We know from history and tradition that of the original twelve apostles, John alone died a natural death. All the others—except Judas, who committed suicide—were executed for their faith. Not one of them was willing to renounce that faith to save his life. Not one was willing to let go of the change that commitment to Jesus had brought into his life and revert to his old way of living.

Why not? Because they knew that the path they were following, as difficult and full of danger as it may have been, was far better than anything they had ever known before. Whatever sacrifice they had to make in order to stay on that path, including suffering and death, was well worth it.

Something Happens to Your World

The second thing that happens when you decide to say "nevertheless" and move out in faith is that *something happens to your world.*

When New Missions first came to Haiti, there were some Haitians who didn't welcome us with open arms. Some were suspicious of our motives. But over time, as they saw our faithful persistence in following the path God had set before us, even those who were most resistant were won over. They saw us doing the same thing day after day: feeding their children, educating them, giving them medical care when they needed it, teaching them about the love of Christ. In other words, we simply kept on "washing and mending our nets" and after a time, the opposition all but disappeared. They knew we had come to Haiti as Christ's representatives, and they trusted us in that. And, because they trusted what we were doing in Christ's name, many of them also came to Christ as Lord.

When you determine that you will say "nevertheless" and persist faithfully along the path God has set before you, your influence will dramatically increase. You will begin to effect circumstances, motivate people, and create new conditions in which God begins to work.

Something Happens to the Ones You Love

The third thing that happens when you decide to say "nevertheless" and follow Jesus is that the lives of your loved ones are changed for the better. The simple reason for this is that God's plans for you are better than any plans you could ever make for yourself. And because they are better for you, they are also better for the people you love: your husband or wife, your children, your parents, your friends, all of those who are important to you, and who truly love you.

You see, God's plans are always better because yours and mine are always selfish to some degree. I'd like to believe that a husband would never make any plans that put his own desires or needs above those of his wife, or vice versa, but I'd have to be a very idealistic person to believe that.

When push comes to shove, most of us are in there pushing and shoving as hard as we can to get what we think is rightfully ours, unless we have made the decision to say, "You know what I want, Lord. You know how self-centered I can be. Nevertheless, I commit myself to doing what you want me to do."

The Bible reminds us again and again that all human beings are selfish and have fallen short of God's perfection. Our selfishness is just a fact of human nature. Therefore, it's only when we try to put our own desires aside and truly follow God's plans for us that we do what is best for those we love.

I might as well admit that there wasn't unanimous rejoicing in my family when my parents made the decision to move to Haiti. For some of us, the feeling was, hey, it's terrific to go down there every once in awhile on a mission trip, but it's not the sort of place you'd want to live. Every year, the United States Coast Guard intercepts thousands of Haitians who try to enter the United States illegally and returns them home. Anyone who's willing to get on board a small sailboat and try to make it more than 700 miles to Florida has to be pretty desperate! In other words, if thousands of people are willing to risk their lives to get *out* of Haiti, then what in the world were we doing working so hard to get *in*?

Now, looking back, the move was one of the best things that could have happened to our family. We've gained much from our Haitian experience:

- We've learned to trust God in every circumstance.
- We've grown together through the pursuit of a common goal.
- Our faith has become more real to us.
- We have grown in character.
- We have grown in compassion for others and in our desire to see the lost come to know Christ.

Will you say "nevertheless" and make a whole-hearted commitment to follow God's plan for your life? If you say yes, life will never be the same for you or the people you love.

—m— —m— —m—

When you commit yourself and begin to act on what God has called you to do, a new force takes hold in your life. Though it may be small at first, it has the potential to grow into whatever God desires it to be, if only you will make the first step of commitment.

Eight

And the Nets Broke!

Simon answered, "Master, we've worked hard all night and haven't caught anything. But because you say so, I will let down the nets." When they had done so, they caught such a large number of fish that their nets began to break.

—Luke 5:5-6

I can just imagine the pandemonium that took place on Lake Gennesaret on that morning long ago.

Who knows whether Peter and the others really thought they would catch any fish? More likely, they were expecting to drag those heavy nets out of the water empty once again. Yes, I'm sure they had a measure of faith, or they wouldn't have gone back out there. And they had hope. But mixed in with faith and hope was doubt, and doubt can be a very powerful thing, especially when it is doubt based on experience. They had already dragged their nets out of the water completely empty, with only a few weeds and other plants tangled in the roping. Based on that experience, it was really kind of silly to expect anything more.

But despite their doubts, they rowed out onto the lake, riding up and down on the small waves stirred up by early morning winds. Then they cast their nets out onto the lake, watching quietly as the ropes sank into the blue-green water.

After a few moments, Peter signaled the others that it was time to pull the nets back into the boats. They all took their usual stations, grabbed hold of the nets and pulled a little. Nothing happened. They pulled again. Nothing. What was going on here? Were they snagged on something?

They were big, strong men, but it took every bit of muscle to pull those nets up to the surface, and when they did, they discovered that those nets were completely loaded with fish, flopping around, full of life and fight! So loaded with fish, in fact, that the nets couldn't hold them, and began to break. Those nets weren't made out of yarn or string. They were knotted together from strong ropes, but they still couldn't hold all the fish!

I like to imagine the apostles beginning to laugh with joy as they tried to cope with the situation. And even though the Bible doesn't tell us, I imagine a crowd may have gathered on the shore, laughing, pointing and shouting:

"Have you ever seen anything like this?"

"No! It's a miracle!"

"How did they catch all those fish?"

"The teacher—Jesus. He told them to put their nets back into the water. And look what happened!"

I believe that as those people began to realize the enormity of what they were seeing, their joy turned to reverence and awe. This Jesus was no mere man. This was not some parlor trick. Nobody had ever seen so many fish in one place before. This was a miracle, the type of event they had heard about, but had never seen. The kind of thing you share with your grandchildren.

But the miracle catch of fish wasn't really about *fish* at all. It was, first of all, a demonstration of what can happen through us when God's Word is obeyed. And it was also a demonstration of God's power to provide for the daily needs of His people.

After seeing what Jesus had done that day, none of the apostles could say, "Well, Lord, I'd like to follow you and become a fisher of men, but if I do that, how am I going to make a living? I mean, I've got to be able to eat and have money for clothes...." Jesus had demonstrated that He was able to provide for their needs at any time. He had proved not only that He could meet their needs, but that He was able "to do immeasurably more than all we ask or imagine" (Ephesians 3:20).

God Can Fill Your Nets

Latter Rain Christian Fellowship, a church in Massachusetts, is pastored by a man named Ernie Frye. For 10 years, Rev. Frye and the members of his congregation were leasing their building on a yearly basis from a large real estate development corporation. Every year, when the time came to renew the lease, the rent went up. And every year the real estate corporation said they were raising the rent because they were planning to make all sorts of improvements to the property in the coming year. But somehow they never got around to making those improvements.

During this same time period, Ernie Frye was the largest monthly supporter of New Missions. A pastor who didn't own a church building for his people was building churches for people he did not know in Haiti. Then about ten years ago, the company offered to sell the building to the congregation for $1.6 million. The church didn't have that kind of money, so they continued paying more than $8,500 per month to lease the property. Sunday after Sunday, they kept praying that God would help them find a way to purchase the property, though that wasn't going to happen short of a miracle.

And then...

Three years later, the news came that the development company that owned the property was going through difficult times and had stopped paying the mortgage. In fact, there were two mortgages on the building, and the development company was more than $750,000 in debt on it. Now the bank that held the first mortgage didn't want to foreclose on a building that was being rented to a church, because that would have been a public relations nightmare. They began looking for a solution. The details were complicated, involving offers, counteroffers, foreclosures, auctions and such. But the end result was that the bank could not collect the mortgage balance from the owner; they sold the mortgage itself to the church for $100,000 and the church foreclosed on its own landlord. That's not a misprint. The same property that had been offered to them for $1.6 million was theirs for less than a tenth of the price.

If you'd like to meet some people who are excited about what the Lord can do, you should go to that church some Sunday morning. Those people know all about nets that break because they can't hold the blessings God has poured into them.

They know that for those who follow and obey Him, God is still in the net-breaking business today!

When we enter into God's plans He pours out the blessing. Speaking through the prophet Malachi, God says, "Test me in this…and see if I will not throw open the floodgates of heaven and pour out so much blessing that you will not have room enough for it" (Malachi 3:10).

The Miracle Truck

When we first began planning our move to Haiti, we needed a truck. So we went to the Worcester Surplus Vehicle Auction and bought one for $500. It was twelve years old, had holes in the floorboards, and on both doors it said, "Worcester Cemetery Department Vehicle 503." In other words, it was no beauty. Then the men from my dad's church got together and gave it a shiny new paint job. They replaced all the tires. And you know what? That truck was still no beauty. Frankly, it looked like it was going to fall apart at any moment.

Nevertheless, my brother Charlie and another missionary, John Vrooman, drove that truck 1500 miles, all the way from Worcester to Miami, where I was going to school. From there, we drove it to the docks and then shipped it on to Haiti.

I'm sure that anyone who might have been watching us at the time would have thought we were foolish to buy that truck. It didn't look like it would survive the trip to Florida, and even if it did, it wasn't likely to last long in Haiti, considering the horrendous conditions of the roads there.

I know that if God had not watched over that truck, it would have been a waste of $500. But He kept it running, even on Haiti's rutted dirt roads. That may not sound like much of a miracle to you, but anyone who had a first-hand view of what that vehicle meant to our ministry in those early days would have a different view. We believe that because we were using the truck for the task God had set before us, He kept it running well past the time it should have been hauled to the junkyard. Because it was a tangible sign of God's blessing, we grew to love that old clunker.

And, because I have seen God's blessings poured out so often, I can say with confidence that it's impossible to underestimate God's power and His desire to bless. I'm convinced that next to seeing a lost soul come into His kingdom, God's greatest joy is pouring out blessings on His children that overflow nets!

Aftermath of a Miracle

I am convinced there is nothing you can do to deserve God's blessing. It is something He gives freely, just as he gives the gift of salvation. But, having said that, I do believe there are some things you can do to stay in a position where He is able to bless you.

Take a look at what happened immediately after the miracle catch of fish:

> When Simon Peter saw this, [the nets breaking because they were so full of fish] he fell at Jesus' knees and said, "Go away from me, Lord; I am a sinful man!" For he and all his companions were astonished at the catch of fish they had taken, and so were James and John, the sons of Zebedee, Simon's partners (Luke 5:8-9).

How do you come to the place where God can lead you beyond yourself, beyond the ordinary and into the destiny that He has planned for you? Learn to live in a state of worship.

We need to have, and hold onto, a vision of *the awesomeness of God.* We must always remember how dependent we are upon Him. Don't make the mistake of thinking that He needs us to worship Him, because He doesn't. He *loves* us, with a greater love than we could ever understand. But He doesn't *need* us. We, on the other hand, need Him very much. Without Him, our lives will be little more than a few thrills, lots of disappointments and empty nets.

I believe that the moment when Peter knelt at Jesus' feet for the first time, his destiny was forever altered. He knelt in acknowledgment of Christ's lordship, putting himself in the proper position of a servant. Likewise, when we acknowledge Christ, not only as Savior but as Lord, we bind our spirit to His Spirit.

When Worship Doesn't Come Easy

How do we keep ourselves in an attitude of worship? I mean worship as a *life posture,* not the Sunday morning thing we do. There are times when it can be very difficult to keep in mind the awesomeness of God, for instance, when you're walking the floor at 2:00 A.M. with a six-month-old who's suffering from an earache!

Remember Ben, the 43-year-old repairman who wants to do something more with his life? He loves God. He really does. But there are times when his love for God is not uppermost in his mind. He's not in a worshipful attitude on Monday morning at 6:00 o'clock, for example, when the alarm goes off, and it's all he can do to drag himself out of bed to face another work week. Or on Tuesday evening at 11:00 P.M., as he crawls into bed after an evening of trying to figure out how to pay all the bills that are due, and his wife tells him that one of the kids needs braces. And then there's Wednesday afternoon, when he's overwhelmed at work, and wondering if the weekend is ever really going to get here.

Ben regrets that the pressures of life sometimes seem to come between him and God. That's one of the reasons he has given such serious thought to going into full-time Christian work. He thinks it would be easier to stay in a worshipful position if he was working for God on a full-time basis. But as any pastor could tell him, that's not always the case. The truth is that we're all working full-time for God, no matter what we do.

Now I am not saying that Ben shouldn't go into full-time Christian work. If that's what God wants him to do, then he should do it. But he has to be sure that he's not doing it for the wrong reasons, or because he has an idealistic notion of what it would mean.

But the question remains: How do you stay focused on Jesus when your kids need a college education? How can you keep your heart fixed on God when people around you who never give Him a second thought breeze through life? How can you stay in a state of worship when you are sick, or going through financial difficulty, or dealing with a job that is non-stop pressure from start to finish every day of the week?

To answer those questions, I'd like to tell you a little bit more about my family and my brother, Tim. I've already mentioned that I have two brothers and a sister. But in between those births, my mom suffered through four miscarriages. In 1972, when she became pregnant with Tim, her doctors scheduled an abortion. They felt that she would never be able to carry the pregnancy to term. One of her miscarriages was at eight months. And it wasn't only the baby's welfare that had them concerned. They were also afraid for my mother's health. They urged her strongly to go against her convictions and have an abortion. They believed it would be the best possible choice for the unborn child, for her personally, and for her other three children who needed her so much.

Reluctantly, my mother decided the doctors were right. One of the physicians was the chief of staff at a leading hospital in

Boston. She would terminate the pregnancy. After making this heart-wrenching decision, one of the first things she did was call her mother to tell her what she had decided.

I was only eleven years old at the time, but I overheard my mother's tearful telephone conversation. As soon as she hung up the phone, I approached her. "Mommy," I asked, "why do you have to have an abortion?"

My mother shared with me, in language I could understand, that the baby in her tummy was very sick. She said the doctors felt certain it was going to die, and they wanted to put it to sleep.

I knew that my mother had lost other babies. That meant there was a chance this one would die, too. But I saw no reason to kill it.

"The other babies died by themselves," I said. "Why don't you just let this baby die naturally, too?"

My mother remembers that my words haunted her all the rest of that day and night. She could not sleep, as my words kept coming back to her.

As the agonizing pain of her lost children came back to her she prayed earnestly for God's guidance, and remembers that, "as I thought about the pain and disappointment, I also remembered the presence of God that had been there during each delivery, comforting me afterward.

"My mind continued to linger over the past. I reflected on the grace I had received after losing each of my babies. With the memory came the realization that there was no need to take matters into my own hands during this pregnancy either. I knew that if this baby died—even late in my pregnancy—God would give me the grace to suffer the loss. For certainly, the God of all comfort would support and give me hope in the tomorrows, just as surely as He had supported me in the yesterdays."

The doctors were not happy with my mother's decision. As far as they were concerned, there was no way the unborn child was going to survive, and they believed my mother had made an irresponsible decision. Still, despite the doctors' dire warnings, my mother prayed that the baby would live, and, as an act of faith, began shopping for maternity clothes.

As her doctors had said it would be, my mom's pregnancy was hard. More than once she had to go into the hospital for an intra-uterine blood transfusion. She spent weeks lying flat on her back in bed. Finally, the baby was born two months premature.

My mother remembers it this way:

> When the baby, born breech, was finally delivered all I could see was a little bluish creature that wasn't breathing. Waiting specialists whisked it away. Then after a few eternally long minutes, [we] received the wonderful news: our four-pound baby son could breathe.
>
> But there were problems. Our little Timothy needed his blood changed, not once, but over and over. It was painful to leave him behind in the hospital when it came time for me to leave. And our frequent visits weren't easy either.

Doctors still didn't think Tim was going to survive. He had to undergo thirty-eight blood exchanges and spent his first two months in the hospital. Even after he came home, doctors weren't confident about his future. There were many health complications, including the fact that he was diagnosed with cerebral palsy, and no one knew if he would ever walk. But my parents kept praying, believing and trusting in God's grace.

Slowly, steadily, he began to improve, and by the time he was ready for school he was an active little boy, normal in every way. Today, you'd never know he had such a difficult babyhood. He's actively involved in the ministry of New Missions, he's an exceptionally talented musician, and moreover, he's a constant reminder of God's grace and love in difficult times.

Because I was only a boy myself, I didn't really understand the anguish my parents went through during the early years of Tim's life. But I knew one thing: they never took their eyes off Jesus. They believed that no matter what happened, the Lord would carry them through, and He did. There were no guarantees of a good outcome, but they knew God was in charge of the situation, they understood something of His eternal love, and they found peace in the knowledge that whatever He did would be the best thing possible.

What would life have been like for them during those difficult months if they had not known the Lord—had they not kept their hearts focused in a worshipful attitude about the awesome power of God. To me, the question is not so much *how* to keep your eyes on the Lord when you're going through difficult times, but, how do people who don't know the Lord make it through challenging times? For when things are at their worst, God's presence can bring the most comfort. God alone can bring peace in the midst of turmoil. He can make sense out of the chaos that comes with day-to-day life on this planet.

In his book, *Abide in Christ*, Andrew Murray says:

> Dear Christian, in affliction abide in Christ. When you see it coming, meet it in Christ; when it is come, feel that you are more in Christ than in it, for He is nearer you than affliction ever can be; when it is passing, still abide in Him....
>
> So shall your times of affliction become your times of choicest blessing—preparation for richest fruitfulness. Led into closer fellowship with the Son of God, and deeper experience of His love and grace—established in the blessed confidence that He and you entirely belong to each other—more completely satisfied with Him and more wholly given up to Him than ever before—with your own will crucified afresh, and the heart brought into deeper harmony with God's will—you shall be a vessel cleansed, meet for the Master's use, prepared for every good work.[6]

That's the way my parents found it to be during the time of their trial, and it's the way I've found it to be in every trial that has come my way since then. Whenever my way seems too challenging, I look at life through eyes of faith.

Augustine said, "I *believe* that I might *understand*." This is true. Keep your eyes on Jesus, even in the midst of trouble and you will come to understand. And when your understanding is enlightened by faith, you discover the joy of the path He has set before you.

Working with Him, Not for Him

Another problem for some people is that they get busy doing things *for* God and totally lose sight of living and working *with* Him.

Earlier, we talked about 22-year-old Joey, who was trying to make up his mind between a career in business or Christian music. Joey dreams of writing and performing songs that are going to change the world. He wants to come up with the right combination of lyrics and music that will impact the masses for Christ.

But if Joey does decide on music, he's going to have to be very careful to keep his focus on Christ. Otherwise, he's likely to find that there's little time for the Lord in his hectic schedule. If he makes it big, he'll spend most of his time on the road, traveling to and from concerts. There will be long days and nights in the recording studio. Interviews. And he'll have to find time to write new songs. If he doesn't watch out, he'll wind up like some pastors I've known, running here and there at full speed, trying to do things for God until he collapses. And then he will realize it's been a long time since he had a heart-to-heart talk with God. He may even wonder where God is keeping Himself these days.

This is the "Martha, Martha" syndrome, as shown in Luke 10:

> As Jesus and his disciples were on their way, they came to a village where a woman named Martha opened her home to him. She had a sister called Mary, who sat at the Lord's feet, listening to what he said. But Martha was distracted by all the preparations that had to be made. She came to him and asked, "Lord, don't you care that my sister has left me to do the work by myself? Tell her to help me!"
>
> "Martha, Martha," the Lord answered, "you are worried and upset about many things, but only one thing is needed. Mary has chosen what is better, and it will not be taken away from her" (vv. 38-42).

Martha was trying to do things for her Lord, and that couldn't be a bad thing. But Jesus said that Mary, who was simply sitting at his feet and listening to Him, had chosen what was better.

Watchman Nee puts it this way:

> It is so easy to become more attached to the gifts of God than to the Giver—and even, I should add, to the work of God than to God Himself.
>
> Let me illustrate. At the present time I am engaged in writing a book. I have finished eight chapters and I have another nine to write, about which I am seriously exercised before the Lord. But if the call to

"Come up hither" [i.e. the rapture] should come and my reaction were to be, "What about my book?" the answer might well be, "All right, stay down and finish it!" That precious thing which we are doing downstairs "in the house" can be enough to pin us down, a peg that holds us to earth.[7]

If you want to have the strength and endurance to continue on the way to your destiny, it is imperative that you stay focused on Christ and rest in Him. Work *with* Him, not *for* Him. Walk alongside of Him, instead of lagging behind or running on ahead, and His blessings will find you.

—✺— —✺— —✺—

Don't ever give up. God is the same now as He was 2,000 years ago. He is still able to do more for us than we can ask, think or imagine. He hasn't changed. His abilities haven't changed. Neither has His concern for His people.

Nine

Building Your Team

Though one may be overpowered, two can defend themselves. A cord of three strands is not quickly broken.

—Ecclesiastes 4:12

O ut on the Sea of Galilee, a man named Simon Peter had the most amazing experience of his life. After hours of futile fishing, he dipped his nets in the water one more time, and they came up so full of fish that they were bursting at the seams.

Because of the overabundance of fish, Peter and the other fishermen who were in his boat couldn't handle the situation by themselves. The Bible tells us, "they signaled their partners in the other boat to come and help them, and they came and filled both boats so full that they began to sink" (Luke 5:7).

What would Peter have done if he had not been part of a team? He would have stood helplessly and watched the nets break, letting the biggest catch of his life swim away.

Teamwork is a very important part of the story of the miracle catch of fish. In fact, the primary reason Jesus was at the lakeside that morning was to begin building His own team. Even though He was the Son of God, full of power and wisdom, He still needed a team; twelve partners who would walk beside Him, assisting in ministry. Twelve men who would be able to watch and learn from Him, and then carry on His life-changing work.

Three of the men who took part in the miracle that day became Jesus' first disciples: Peter, James and John. It's interesting, I think, that these three, who began their walk with Christ while witnessing His astonishing power over nature, became His closest companions. During the years of Christ's earthly ministry, they were almost always by His side—the only disciples He allowed to be in the room when He raised Jairus' daughter from the dead, the only ones to witness the transfiguration, the ones He asked to pray for Him in the Garden of Gethsemane.

We might say that they were like Jesus' team within a team— His inner circle.

You Need a Team

In order to become everything God wants us to be, you and I need a team to help us. Everyone needs "a team," from the child on the playground to the chief financial officer of a Fortune 500 corporation. Just as Jesus hand-picked twelve men to be His apostles, we can consciously look for people to serve as members of our personal spiritual support teams. If you have the wisdom, strength and counsel of a good team, you can find great strength and encouragement on the path God has called you to follow.

When Jesus left the lakeshore that day, He continued building His team. He chose men whose traits balanced each other. Sometimes they looked like opposites. If He'd wanted men who were all alike, He wouldn't have picked Matthew, who collected taxes for the occupying Roman forces, to work alongside Simon the Zealot, who worked for the overthrow of the Roman government! Those two weren't likely to have a whole lot in common, but Jesus needed the strengths that each brought to the table, and so both were on His team.

Take a closer look at the men Jesus chose to be His apostles, and you'll see that they were about as divergent as twelve people could possibly be. But Jesus carefully chose just the men He needed, including Judas.

For the past 2,000 years, Jesus has continued to build His team. Acts 2 tells us that in the early days of the church, "the Lord added to their number daily those who were being saved" (Acts 2:47). The "adding" has continued throughout the centuries. If you are a Christian, you are a member of Christ's body, which means that you are a member of His team.

There Is Safety in Numbers

Who would you say is the most respected Christian leader of our day? Many would say Billy Graham. If I asked 100 people that question, probably 90 would choose him. And with good reason. He has been steady in his service for God for more than 50 years. During that time he has managed to avoid the excesses that have damaged or toppled other ministries. Although he has been one of America's best-known personalities for decades, he is still the same humble servant of God who first began holding tent meetings back in the 1940s. There has never been a hint of scandal with Billy Graham or his organization.

Why? Obviously it has to do with the character of Dr. Graham himself. I believe there are very few people who could have spent as much time in the spotlight and come away less affected. Clearly, Billy Graham knows who he is in Christ, and has a very proper understanding of himself as God's servant. But I also believe that much of the credit must go to the excellent team Dr. Graham has built. He has never been an autocratic leader. Instead, he has sought out the advice and counsel of men and women he trusts. His wife, Ruth, is a very important part of that team, which is as it should be for any committed Christian couple.

Where Is Your Team?

Every Christian needs "team" members—a few people who can support you, encourage you and offer counsel. My own team consists of support staff at work, advisers, a Christian attorney who gives me invaluable legal advice, and a CPA who helps with financial counsel. My pastor is on my team. So is my wife. These people are available to me almost any time I need them. At times, I've had to call one of them at three in the morning and say, "I've got a problem." These friends are committed. They've been willing to get out of bed when necessary and do what's needed to help me. I would have a very difficult time as a leader without the support of my team.

Everyday people who want to fulfill God's plan for their lives also benefit from a support team in the most practical of ways.

Janie felt God calling her to start a neighborhood Bible club for kids. She called her pastor and a close friend, Louise, who became her prayer warriors and her "advisory council."

Les heard the Lord's call to step from his 20-year career into full-time ministry. He phoned four pastors who could advise and encourage him as he made the transition. More importantly, he decided to keep them "on-call" as his field advisers, so they could help him think through the questions and problems he'd no doubt encounter in serving a church. He knew several pastors who had tried to go it alone, without close confidants, and who had burned-out or quit the ministry altogether.

Bob, an auto mechanic, wanted to present a more effective Christian witness to the guys in the garage. He sought out the counsel of the head of his church's evangelism committee, and became involved with a group of like-minded men and women who gathered for a prayer breakfast one day a week. He developed strong relationships with supportive people who were able to advise and encourage him as he strove to be a better representative of Christ in the workplace.

Whoever you are, whatever you want to do, you need a team!

When should you start building your team? Right now.

Why do you need a team? Because a team gives you:

Safety. A good team will keep you from running in the wrong direction. Earlier in the book, I introduced you to Sally, the young homemaker who, although she understands the importance of being a wife and mother, wants to do something more with her life. But what? One of her dreams is to get involved with a charitable organization—Christian if possible—and invest the talents God has given her in making life better for the less fortunate. Sally needs a team to help her sort through the various opportunities that are open to her, and discover which are really suited to her talents and temperament. If Sally is drawn in a particular direction, but all of her team members feel that she'd be making a mistake, she would be well-served to heed their advice.

Support. When you build your team, you are not looking for people who all think alike, or even for people who think like you do. Instead, you're looking for men and women who are going to provide the necessary balance to your personality. If you're impulsive, look for someone who is more thoughtful and introspective. If you're the type who can't seem to hold onto a dollar, you probably want someone on your team who has demonstrated an ability to save and invest. In other words, you need people who are strong where you are weak, so they can support you in areas where you tend to struggle. You don't want a bunch of yes-men and women, but you do want people who can take a clear-eyed look at the situation when you're feeling down or discouraged, and say, "You're doing great. Don't give up."

Assistance. Bill Gates, the multi-billionaire founder of Microsoft, says that if you're in a position to hire people, the best thing you can do is hire the most brilliant people you can find. You don't even have to know why you're hiring them. Let them find out what they're good at, let them do it, and you can't lose. Jack Welch, CEO of General Electric, said having the right team is more important than having the right strategy. Why? Because if you have the right team, it will help you create the right strategy. But if you combine a great strategy with a terrible team, you won't get anywhere. The people on your team can either propel you forward or hold you back, so it's paramount that you ask the right people to be on your team. More about that in a moment.

Personal accountability. Earlier, I mentioned Billy Graham's team. Part of that team's purpose is to hold him accountable. You may say, "Wait a minute…this is Billy Graham we're talking about!" Yes, it is. But he is still accountable to the rules that have been established by his organization. I don't know who you are. You may be the most important person in your city. That doesn't matter when it comes to accountability. Everyone needs to be accountable to *someone.*

Mark is a businessman who has a history of making poor financial decisions. Because he recognized his weakness in this area of life, he set up an "accountability group" consisting of people whose judgment he respects including an accountant, his pastor, his brother-in-law, and several other Christian businessmen. Whereas he once had a tendency to act impulsively and recklessly in his financial affairs, he now meets with his team at least once a month to seek their counsel, and he is much better because of it.

Being accountable to people whose judgment you trust can go a long way toward removing stress and anxiety from your life. A good team will help you make important decisions, hold you accountable regarding how you carry out those decisions, and then help you analyze your performance after the fact. As your team keeps you accountable, you can be more confident that you are moving steadily forward on the path God wants you to follow.

How Do You Build Your Team?

How do you find people to serve on your team?

First, you may find them in your *family.*

Then, at *church.*

Third, among *friends and neighbors.*

Next, in your circle of *co-workers.*

And finally, look for *anyone who has the talents and abilities you need to balance your own skills.*

Ten years ago I was asked to speak in two churches in New York. At the time, I hadn't done much public speaking, and I wasn't at all confident or comfortable with it. I called my brothers, Charlie and Timmy, and said, "I really need you to go with me." Both of them were busy, but I reminded them that in Ecclesiastes it says a cord of three strands cannot easily be broken. "If you guys will come with me, I know something great will happen."

As I recall, Charlie, especially, had to put himself out to give me what I needed, and I've always been grateful that he was willing to do it.

As it turned out, we did have a great victory. I preached in those two little churches to warm, receptive audiences. But the best thing about that trip was the way it bound us brothers together. Ever since then, whenever one of us has been in need, our rallying cry has been, "The Three Brothers!" In fact, one year for my birthday, Charlie, who loves nautical things, gave me a framed painting of a sailing ship named "The Three Brothers." I treasure that painting as a symbol of the support we give each other. My brothers are a very important part of my personal team. We stand up for each other in every situation. Our unity is more valuable to us than any lesser issue that comes up between us.

After your family, *church* is a wonderful place to find people you want for your team. But in order to find them, you've got to be involved in a church where God is honored and the people are serious about wanting to follow Him.

First of all, I'm talking about pastors, teachers, elders, deacons; men and women who are in positions of spiritual leadership within the church. The Bible tells us that God "gave some to be apostles, some to be prophets, some to be evangelists, and some to be pastors and teachers, to prepare God's people for works of service so that the body of Christ may be built up" (Ephesians 4:11-12). I believe that people who are in positions of authority within a God-honoring, Bible-believing church receive their authority from God. And because of that, I also believe that God has given them special gifts of wisdom and guidance, which He expects them to use to provide counseling and guidance to the other members of the congregation. It is also important to have on your team people who have demonstrated a large degree of spiritual maturity.

But when I say you can find people for your team at church, I am not talking *only* about those who are in positions of authority. Church is a great place to meet other Christians who have the particular skills, strengths and personality traits your team requires.

The members of the church make up your extended family, they are your brothers and sisters in Christ. No matter what it is that you feel God is calling you to do, it is almost certain you will find someone in your church who can give you effective guidance and counsel. God expects the members of His body to support and care for one another. God built His church not only to be a place of worship, but also to be a place where we can establish relationships with other people who share our faith. Certainly, God is concerned about our relationship with Him, but He is also concerned about our relationships with other Christians.

Earlier, I introduced you to Ann, who, as she approaches her "golden years," wants to do something more with her life.

The more she thinks about it, the more she feels certain that God wants her to begin a writing and speaking ministry to younger women. As she looks around herself at church on Sunday morning, she sees a number of people who could help her achieve that goal:

There's Joan, the pastor's wife. She has done some speaking and teaches a ladies Bible class in the sanctuary on Wednesday mornings. She should be able to share from her valuable experience.

And speaking of valuable experience, there's Mrs. Smith, who is nearly 90, and one of the founding members of the congregation. She's feeble now, but her mind is sharp, and she would be a great addition to Ann's team. Not only because she has more than

65 years of experience ministering to other women in the church, but because everyone knows she's one of the most dynamic "prayer warriors" you could ever hope to have on your side.

Sitting behind Mrs. Smith, there's Paul, who works for an advertising agency. His expertise would be important when it came to developing brochures and flyers to acquire and announce speaking engagements.

Two pews in back of him, there's Roberta, who always has something insightful to say. She has much to offer in common sense. She's the kind of person who would be a good asset for anybody's team.

Then there's Rita, a woman about Ann's age, who has had some beautiful pieces published in the church bulletin. It's obvious to Ann that she and Rita both have an interest in ministering to younger women. If they joined forces, they could probably do something much greater than either one of them could do alone.

As she continues looking around her, Ann sees a number of other men and women who she would like to enlist as members of this particular team. Now, as I mentioned earlier, most of us need not one team, but several different teams to assist us in the various areas of life. Look around your church, and see if you don't find a number of people who would be invaluable members of your team, people whose friendship and support could help you in a variety of ways.

Another good place to find people for your team(s) is at *work*.

Before Peter, James and John became apostles, they were co-workers—fishermen who sailed the waters of Lake Gennesaret together. I wonder if they ever knew the potential that existed within each other or, if like so many modern workers, they simply worked together, without knowing much about each other. Yes, I know that James and John were brothers, but I wonder whether they ever hung out with Peter after the day's fishing was done. Perhaps not. But after their encounter with Christ, those men were drawn together in a dynamic and powerful way that helped turn the world upside down. I can imagine John turning to James as he listened to Peter preach the first Gospel sermon on the Day of Pentecost (Acts 2), and saying, "Can you believe this guy? All those years of fishing with him, and I never knew he could preach like that! Just goes to show you…you never know!"

I talked about the importance of getting to know your neighbors. It's also important to get to know the people you work with. You might be surprised at the strengths and talents you'll find hidden beneath the surface, if you take the time and make the effort to find them.

Now, some final advice about building your team: *Look for anyone who has the talents and abilities you need.*

Suppose you want to start a ministry, but you're not sure how to go about it, and don't know anyone else who's started the same type of organization. Find someone who does know. Go to the library and do some research. Use the Internet. And then when you find the person who has the expertise you need, write him a letter, explain what you're planning to do, and ask if they would agree to be on your team. The worst they can do is say no. The best they can do is say yes, and possibly become a tremendous asset to you.

Now, that leads me to an important question: How do you go about asking people to be on your team? Sometimes it's a formal procedure. For example, Ann wants Joan, the preacher's wife, to be on her team. She calls her and says, "I think God is calling me to start a ministry to younger women, and I'm trying to put together a team to help me get that started. I'd really appreciate it if you would be willing to be on that team."

Joan will probably have a lot of questions: What do you need me to do? How much time would it take? Why did you ask me to be on your team, and so on.

Some situations, like Ann's, require a more formal approach to team-building. That's true, too, if you're doing something like putting together an accountability team to meet with you twice a month. The people in that group will need to know exactly what you are expecting of them, and they will have to have the opportunity to accept or reject your invitation to be a part of your team. Suppose you're looking for an older, wiser person in your church to mentor you in a particular area. Again, in that situation, it would be wise to be completely open and honest about what you're doing, for example, "It would mean a lot to me if you could have lunch with me at least once a month. I know I could really learn from you."

On other occasions, your team may be a loose, informal affair, with the members of your team not really knowing they are on your team. There's no reason for them to be "official" team members. There are no meetings or anything like that. Your team is simply a group of people you know you can count on for support and guidance when you need it.

However you go about it, God wants you to build a team. And you build the team by establishing strategic relationships everywhere you go.

—∿—　—∿—　—∿—

> *Be open and eager to find others who will join with you as good and faithful teammates to help you reach the destiny God has in mind for you.*

Ten

"Come and Follow Me..."

Then Jesus said to Simon, "Don't be afraid; from now on you will catch men." So they pulled their boats up on shore, left everything and followed him.
—Luke 5:10b-11

*W*hen people ask me, "George, what is God doing in the world today?" I tell them that He's doing the same thing He's always done. He's calling His people out. Look through the Bible and you'll see how He called His people out of complacency and into a greater degree of service. People like Moses. Deborah. Gideon. Elijah. Jeremiah. And so many others who were willing to forsake all and follow Him wherever He wanted them to go. People like you and me.

God May Call You All the Way to Haiti

I don't know specifically what God wants you to do with your life. But whatever it is, I know He is calling each of us to step out of self-centeredness, out beyond our old routines, and into a life centered in Him. When that happens, life becomes an adventure, as He leads us into situations where we are dependent upon His grace and wisdom.

When my dad was growing up in an Italian immigrant family in Boston, there was no reason to think he'd ever set foot on

Haitian soil. It was more likely that he would spend all of his life in New England, living and dying surrounded by generations of the DeTellis family. But when Jesus said, "Come and follow me," both Dad and Mom followed Him all the way to the poorest island in the Caribbean.

Following Jesus Every Day

Sometimes you have to take big steps when you're trying to follow Jesus. You have to move your family to Haiti, or begin an entirely new kind of ministry. Other times, you have to be willing to follow Him in the little details of everyday life.

Paula and I spent our honeymoon in Europe, where we traveled from Paris to Rome by train. In the sleeping car right next to us was an elderly Italian couple on their way back home to Rome from Paris. Achille was a short, commanding man with a full head of gray hair. He told me he'd been in Paris to see if doctors there could determine the cause of the severe headaches that had been tormenting him off and on for months. Sadly, after running a battery of tests, French doctors told him they were every bit as baffled as were his doctors in Rome.

Achille and Chivada told me that he had served as a tank commander under Mussolini during World War II, been captured by the British in North Africa, and sent to a POW camp in India, where he learned to speak English. After the war, he returned to Italy, where he taught school, specializing in English and literature, and also became a chess champion.

Achille was obviously an intelligent, well-read man. In the course of our conversation, I asked him about his favorite books, and was surprised when he asked me if I had ever read Bertrand Russell's *Why I Am Not a Christian.* He said that book had changed his life because it was "so freeing...so liberating."

At that instant, I knew why God had put Paula and me in the sleeping car next to Achille and his wife. This man was 72 years old. He was suffering from headaches for which doctors could not find a reason. There was a good chance he was going home to die. He had read a book which had caused him to renounce faith in Christ, and now God wanted me to try to reach him with the truth, before it was forever too late.

Paula and I both tried to talk to him a little bit about the Lord that night, but although he was gracious, we didn't seem to be making much headway. In fact, I could see that both he and his wife were becoming irritated by our attempts at witnessing, and so we said good evening and went back to our sleeping car. But I didn't sleep *that* night. Instead, as the train rumbled through the Italian alps, I lay in the darkness thinking about Achille, praying for him, and wondering what I could do or say that might make him reconsider his need for Jesus.

All the next morning, I kept looking for a way to work Jesus into the conversation in a natural, comfortable way, but it didn't come. Almost before I knew it, we were standing in the train station in Rome, telling each other goodbye. Before we went our separate ways, I asked Achille if he could help me call an aunt of mine who lives in the city. It was a natural request, since it wasn't immediately apparent to me how to use the Italian telephones.

Achille graciously said he'd be happy to help me. But as God would have it, my aunt wasn't home.

"Well, what are you going to do now?" Achille asked.

"Oh, I don't know," I shrugged. "I guess we'll just wait here until she gets home."

He swept his right hand through the air in a dismissive gesture.

"There is no reason to do that," he said. "Why don't you and your lovely wife come home with us. We would be delighted to have you for dinner."

"Oh, no, we couldn't…." I started to protest that we couldn't think of troubling them in that way. But then I stopped and listened for a moment, and I felt certain that God wanted us to go.

We were all loaded into a taxicab, winding our way up one of the seven hills of the Eternal City. Finally, we pulled up in front of a beautiful home at the very top of the hill. Achille explained that it was his brother's house, and that the whole family was gathering there tonight for dinner.

It was an amazing house, full of flowers, beautiful art, and marble floors. What's more, Paula and I got the welcome of our lives. Everyone acted like we were long-lost American cousins, and we felt very much at ease.

But there was one thing that didn't seem to belong in that house, and it caught my eye the minute I walked through the door. It was a poster.

…of Worcester, Massachusetts, *my hometown!* There it was, framed in glass, hanging on the living room wall. It was one of those stylized maps—I'm sure you've seen them—that has all the streets along with the various businesses, churches, schools, a caricaturist's bird's-eye view of the city.

My mouth fell open when I saw it, and I practically shouted, "Hey! That's my hometown!"

"Really," Achille laughed. "I have family there. Cousins."

"Where do they live?"

He pointed at the poster and gave an address and phone number. As it turned out, his cousins lived just around the corner from Paula and me. God, in His wisdom, had sent me half-way around the world to witness to a man whose cousins were practically neighbors of mine back in Massachusetts!

Achille had been gracious before, but that amazing "coincidence" really caused the barriers to fall. Before the evening was over, I asked him if I could pray with him about his headaches, and he welcomed the offer. Paula and I had a chance to talk to him some more about the Lord as he drove us to my aunt's house. And even though he was not willing at that time to give his life to Christ, he was at least open and willing to hear what we had to say.

Once we returned to the States, I sent him an Italian-language New Testament, and we exchanged a few letters. I got to explain to him more fully what I believe and why I believe it.

Sadly, I have not heard from him in quite some time. But I have the satisfaction and joy of knowing that because I was obedient to God, and went where He wanted me to go, Gospel seeds were planted in Achille's heart.

Have You Counted the Cost?

If you want to uncover the destiny that God has planned for you, it is imperative that you be willing simply to follow Jesus, wherever He leads you. To do so, there is a cost involved. Mark Bailey writes:

> Before we sign up to be Jesus' disciples, we have to count the cost. And just what does it cost to follow Jesus?
>
> Everything!
>
> Jesus used two little stories, one of building and one of battle, to tell us what it means to count the cost. Then he concluded: "In the same way, any of you who does not give up *everything* he has cannot be my disciple" (Luke 14:33 NIV, emphasis mine).

You see, the cost of following Christ is everything. But the rewards! Ah, the rewards are heavenly. Jim Elliot said it well: "He is no fool who gives up what he cannot keep to gain what he cannot lose."[8]

Sometimes it hurts when Jesus tells you to give up something you really want to hold on to. Like a brand-new bicycle.

Let me explain: for several years, I have sponsored a young man in Haiti named Wisnel Joseph. Wisnel is the oldest child in a large, poor family. His father died when Wisnel was a young boy, so ever since then, he has been saddled with the role of "man of the house."

Wisnel is a bright young man who became one of the top students in our elementary school and then went on to excel in our high school. A couple of years ago, a church in California gave bicycles to all the kids in the high school. Those bikes were a wonderful gift, because those kids had to walk for five miles, each way, everyday to get to the high school, including Wisnel. He rode his bike everywhere for months...and then I got a letter from him telling me how very sad he was to have to tell me that the bicycle was broken.

I knew I'd be visiting Haiti within a couple of months, so I figured I'd wait and look into the situation when I was there. Meanwhile, I had a brand new Schwinn sitting in my garage. It was the kind of bike I had always wanted when I was a boy, but had never been able to afford. It was bright red, a three-speed with handle-grip brakes, a beautiful, beautiful bike, and I loved it.

Well, as I knew it would, business took me to Haiti, and my first day there I encountered Wisnel on the path at the mission.

"Ti George," he asked, "what is your vision for my bicycle? I have to walk to the high school every day, and it is very far." (Some of the kids in Haiti call me Ti George, because it means "little George." There's Pastor George—my dad—and me, Ti George.)

"I'll tell you what, Wisnel," I answered. "Paula and I will come to your village today, and we'll see what we can do about your bicycle."

Well, Wisnel's bicycle was a mess. The sprocket was bent and twisted to the point that the chain wouldn't stay on. Ballbearings were missing. Basically, there was no way to fix it.

He needed a new one.

I immediately thought of that beautiful red Schwinn. But it was mine!

That gentle, yet persistent voice spoke to my soul: "He needs it more than you do."

I sighed.

"Wisnel," I said, "you're right. You need a new bicycle. And I know just where I can get you one."

"You do?"

"Yes. And as soon as I get home, I'll send it to you."

So that's what I did. When I returned to the States, I boxed up that gorgeous red bicycle and shipped it off to Haiti. You may be thinking, "Big deal! It was only a bike." That's right. But it was more than a bicycle to me. It was a representation of a childhood dream. It was precious. But God said, "I want you to give it up," and I knew I needed to obey, no matter how much I wanted to fight it.

Now, let me ask you—is there something Jesus is asking you to give up?

Perhaps it is a cherished dream you have always had, but one that is not in line with God's perfect will for you.

It may be an unhealthy relationship with someone who is keeping you from fulfilling God's will for your life. Perhaps an over-attachment to possessions or a position.

God may be asking you to lay your pride, your self-esteem, your independent spirit, or your self-image on the altar.

Whatever it is, the most important thing is to strive to hear what He is saying, and then, having heard, to obey. That's really what following Christ is all about: *Obedience*.

Follow Him in All Things

A friend of mine, a fellow missionary named Tony, tells of the time he was visiting a small Haitian village, and a woman ran up to him, thrust her infant into his arms, and begged him, with tears in her eyes, to pray for the baby.

"My baby's sick! My baby's sick!" she kept shouting.

Tony could tell immediately that the child was burning with fever.

"You've got to get him to a doctor," he said.

"No! You pray for him! Please!"

In Haiti, when children are sick, their parents will sometimes attach voodoo pouches to their clothing in an attempt to ward off the evil influences that they believe are tormenting them. This woman had pinned several such pouches inside her infant's little shirt. Tony was on the spot. Naturally, he felt that the child needed to go to the clinic. But in his spirit, He felt God urging him to pray. Only he wasn't going to do it if this woman was going to try using Voodoo at the same time.

"I'll pray for your baby," he said, "but only if you'll take all those voodoo pouches off. Otherwise, you'll say that voodoo healed your baby."

"All right! I will take them off! But please...pray now!"

As the mother quickly removed the pouches, Tony prayed fervently for the little boy. When he finished, the woman thanked him, with tears streaming down her face, and returned home to await the evidence of God's healing power.

The next day, Tony was back in that village, and when the woman saw him she came running up, laughing and shouting, to tell him that her baby had been healed. And she gave all the glory to Jesus Christ. That little boy could have died. And that would have been a disaster not only for the baby and his mother, but for Tony as well, because he probably would have been blamed for the death. But Tony heard what God was telling him to do. He obeyed without question. As a result, Jesus received praise and honor in that village.

He Gave Up His Life, and Found His Destiny

History records the heroic stories of many men and women who have been willing to obey God's call without question and who have continued washing and mending their nets day after day, year after year, despite the costs involved.

Today, one person in particular comes to mind. He is a man whose life has always been an inspiration to Christians, and particularly missionaries, all over the world.

David was born into a poor family. His parents struggled to provide their children with basic necessities like food and clothing. By the time David was ten years old, things had reached such a desperate state that he had to drop out of school and go to work full-time in a factory. He had to be at work every morning at 6 A.M. and worked twelve-hour days at hard labor. By the time he left for home at night, his back ached, his fingers were sore and his mind was numb with exhaustion.

Still, he was an incredibly bright boy who was determined to get an education. Even though most of the money he made went directly to his parents, he used a small portion of his very first paycheck to buy a book on Latin grammar, which he studied diligently. He also began attending classes at night.

That pattern continued through the early years of his life. He worked during the day, attended school at night, and spent whatever free time he had studying medicine, science and literature on his own. He worked his way through college, and then medical school, where he was noted as one of the very best and brightest in his class.

His professors felt that young David had an unlimited future. It seemed certain that his days of poverty and need would soon be left behind. As a successful physician, he would surely be able to live "the good life."

But right around his twentieth birthday, David read a Christian book that moved him deeply. He surrendered himself to Christ, and, as he put it, "In the glow of love which Christianity inspires, I soon resolved to devote my life to the alleviation of human suffering."

He came to believe that God was calling him to the mission field—perhaps to China. He turned his attention to the study of Chinese history and culture because he felt he would spend his life in service to the Lord there. But after several months, that door was slammed shut. David might have shrugged it off and said, "Well, at least I tried. I guess I'll just stay home, practice medicine, buy a big house, and seek an active role in my church." Instead, he turned his attention to Africa.

But again, months passed, and it seemed that he was no closer to his dream of going to the mission field than when he had first felt God's call on his life. Some people tend to let the "wild dreams" of their youth fade away with time, and he certainly could have done that as he worked in the hospitals of his native Great Britain. But he would not give up his dream, no matter what anyone thought or said.

David persisted, the door finally opened, and he made his way to Africa, where he remained for almost all of the last 33 years of his life.

He gave up so much to go to Africa.

In his native London, David could have lived in a fine house with servants and all the latest conveniences. In Africa, he lived in a series of grass huts with dirt floors. The rain poured through the ceilings. The wind blew through the walls, but he was joyful because he knew he was exactly where God wanted him to be.

In London, he could have known the elegance and safety of "proper society." In Africa, he endured numerous bouts with diseases such as malaria, underwent spear attacks by hostile tribes, and braved encounters with head-hunters, cannibals and ferocious wild animals.

Much of the time he was in Africa, David's life was at great risk. He traveled far into the interior of what was, at the time, completely uncharted territory seeking souls for Christ. He learned a number of native languages and dialects in order to speak to the African people directly about the love of God. He was among the first to see the importance of raising up indigenous leaders for the African church.

Along the way, he produced the first maps of much of Africa, and, because he was a man of science, catalogued the plant and animal life he encountered on his journeys.

In a time when many European men were building their own kingdoms in Africa, David was there to build the kingdom that stands on the eternal love of Christ. Many were in Africa to steal and rob, but David was there only to give. For more than thirty years, he was a friend and champion of the African people. For example, he was outspoken in his opposition to the cruelty of the slave trade, which was common throughout much of Africa at the time.

When death finally came for David, it did not come in the comfort of a hospital bed, but through illness while on yet another dangerous expedition to reach the lost for Christ.

By this time he had become a hero in his native Britain, and the government asked for his body to be returned so it could be entombed in a place of honor in Westminster Abbey. David's African friends respectfully carried his body hundreds of miles to the coast so it could be placed aboard a ship and returned to Europe.

But those Africans knew something very special about David.

His body might belong to Britain. But he had told them time and time again that his heart belonged to Africa. It was there, in the midst of trials, struggles and personal loss, including the death of his beloved wife, that he had found joy, peace and fulfillment.

And so today, if you visit the tomb of Dr. David Livingstone in Westminster Abbey, you will find an inscription explaining that the great man's heart is not buried there, but rather in Africa, because it belonged to that continent and its people!

It would be more correct to say his heart belonged to God, for it was his love for God that took him to Africa, and to the fulfillment of his heart's desires.

What did David Livingstone give up to spend his life in Africa? So very much.

What did David Livingstone gain by going to Africa? He gained the unexplainable joy that comes to those who are willing to follow God wherever He may lead, those who continuously keep their nets clean and in good repair, praying all the while, "Not my will, Lord, but thine!"

Follow Christ All the Way

David Livingstone was a man who took hold of Paul's admonition, "Run in such a way as to get the prize" (1 Corinthians 9:24b). He could say, along with the apostle, "I press on to take hold of that for which Christ Jesus took hold of me. Brothers, I do not consider myself yet to have taken hold of it. But one thing I do: Forgetting what is behind and straining toward what is ahead, I press on toward the goal to win the prize for which God has called me heavenward in Christ Jesus" (Philippians 3:12-14).

How far are you willing to follow Christ? Would you follow all the way to the cross? As Jesus said, "If anyone would come after me, he must deny himself and take up his cross daily and follow me. For whoever wants to save his life will lose it, but whoever loses his life for me will save it" (Luke 9:23-24).

It is only when we are willing to spend our lives that we can really begin to live. The most menial task, when done for Christ with the certainty that it is what He wants us to do, can be a source of great personal satisfaction and fulfillment. The routine that seems confining and stifling without Christ becomes, with Him, an exciting and liberating adventure. Be willing to lose your life, and you will find it.

———

Earlier in this book, I introduced you to four people who are trying to find God's destiny for their lives: Sally, Ben, Ann and Joey. The future stretches before them. But how will they spend their lives? As they continue to wash and mend their nets on a daily basis, as they commit themselves completely to Christ, determined to follow Him wherever He may lead them, the result will be absolutely glorious.

Keep mending and washing your nets. And when the Lord speaks to you, let down your nets. Catch your destiny!

When you determine to follow Jesus wherever He leads you, you begin to move steadily toward the destiny for which you were created. Jesus is calling you today, saying, "Come, follow me, be my disciple."

Footnotes

1. Bruce Larson, *Faith for the Journey* (San Francisco: Harper & Row, 1983) pp. 35-36.
2. Ibid., pp. 34-35.
3. Ibid., pp. 110-111.
4. Ibid., pp. 41-42.
5. Watchman Nee *The Normal Christian Life* (Wheaton, IL: Tyndale House Publishers, 1977) pp. 254-255.
6. Andrew Murray *Abide In Christ* (New Canaan, CT: Keats Publishing, Inc., 1973) p. 97.
7. Watchman Nee, p. 257.
8. Mark Bailey, *To Follow Him* (Sisters, OR: Multnomah Books, 1997) pp. 124-125.

If you would like to correspond with George DeTellis, Jr. personally or obtain more information regarding short-term mission opportunities or how to sponsor a child, please write to:

NEW Missions
P.O. Box 2727
Orlando, FL 32802

or call:

(407) 240-4058

You can also visit our web site at:

http://www.newmissions.org

or email:

george@newmissions.org